FOUNDED ON THE ROCK – JESUS CHRIST

Founded on the Rock – Jesus Christ

Harold Deane Thomason Akins

Harold Deane Akins

Autobiography of the Co-founder
and History of the Renowned
Savannah Christian Preparatory School

BONAVENTTURE
books
SAVANNAH

FOUNDED ON THE ROCK – JESUS CHRIST

Library of Congress Control Number: 2006940207
ISBN: 978-0-9724224-5-1
First Edition, January 2007
Printed in Canada
Published in the United States of America

DEDICATION

This book is dedicated to the members of my family who have enriched my life immeasurably and without whom this book could not have been written:

My son, George, Jr., and my daughter-in-law, Barbara.

My two granddaughters and their families:

Patrice and Michael Liburdi	Christi Hice
Sean Liburdi	Dustin Hice
Eric Liburdi	Jordan Hice
	Carly Hice

In addition, this book is dedicated to the current Headmaster of Savannah Christian Preparatory School Roger Yancey and his wife, Ruth Ann. Mr. Yancey is a man of vision and action. It pleases me to see they have taken the school to new heights. The future looks brighter than ever under their leadership.

CONTENTS

Dedication v

Preface 8

PART ONE: THE EARLY YEARS

Love and Marriage 11

My First Trip to the Ocean 15

My Illness 17

My First Airplane Ride 19

My First Trip To New York – A Teenager Goes to the Big Apple
    and on to Marriage 21

More Early Years – A Few Small Accomplishments That Were Big
    To Me 23

An Unusual Graduation and Continuing Education 27

My First Job and First Vacation 30

My New Birth – A Big Step That Would Chart My Life 32

PART TWO: PLANTING AND REAPING

Union Mission, INC. 35

I Joined George in the Work of the Union Mission 40

International Union Of Gospel Missions 41

George Jr. Arrives 43

Mission Youth Camp 47

Beginning of the Evangelical Bible Institute, Now Savannah
    Christian Preparatory School 56

Europe In 1957 76

Mexico and Guatemala 81

Camping With My Grands and Their Girl Friend 90

Above and Beyond the Call of Duty 91

PART THREE: YEARS OF CHANGE

Purchase of Property 94

After Savannah Christian School 95

Our Move to the Landings On Skidaway Island 97

George and I and . . .Golf 99

Egypt and Israel 101

Fiftieth Wedding Anniversary 112

New Zealand and Australia 116

Later Years 124

Europe 2000 125

My Precious Pets 133
Alumni Meetings of Students From the 1950s 135

PART FOUR: FOREIGN MISSION TRIPS
Japan 138
Rice: A Food For All Seasons 151
Taiwan 152
Kenya and Kibera 2003 157
Haiti 174

PART FIVE: LATER ON
Alaska 185
Why Me? 190
Final Thoughts 191
After Thoughts 195

PREFACE

Psalms 119:105. Thy word is a lamp unto my feet, and a light unto my path.

I have learned that without the Lord I am nothing. His blessings have given me a life worth talking and writing about.

When I was in Taipei, Taiwan working in the American Village at Christ's College, Barbara White opened her heart and home to all twelve of us who came from the United States and Canada as missionaries.

One day Barbara told me that I have had such an unusual life I should write a book about it. My reply was I never thought about that, but I would pray about it.

After praying about it, on the plane from Taipei to Narita in Japan, I outlined the divisions I would make and penciled in some notes.

I felt others on a similar Christian path could benefit from the story of my life, including my ministry over the past seventy years – stories about the Union Mission, the Bible clubs, the Mission Youth Camp, and the Evangelical Bible Institute – now Savannah Christian Preparatory School, my missionary trips and personal adventures around the world. I believe learning of my successes and backsteps will shorten the time others spend achieving their similar aspirations and goals. All of my life is a wonderful testimony of God's love and care for me.

I'll make a book of memories to encourage readers to seek a deeper spiritual experience of commitment to our Lord Jesus Christ, who loved us and gave His life for us.

I hope that through reading this book, my family and friends will diligently and humbly seek to follow our Lord and Savior Jesus Christ whom to know aright is life eternal.

It is said of Oscar de la Renta, the famous French fashion designer, that he possessed a restless nature and the drive to take on new challenges typical of a man half his age. I believe that could also be said about me.

Psalms 71:7-9 says, *"I am a wonder unto many, but Thou art my strong refuge. Let my mouth be filled with Thy praise and Thy honor all the day. Cast me not off in the time of old age, forsake me not when my strength faileth."*

I have learned that "Age is a State of Mind."

Who would ever believe that life after 80 could be so fantastic. Life began again for me after I became an octogenarian.

Age has posed no impediments on me.

I want to express my deepest thanks to all my friends who encouraged and helped me in so many ways. God bless you – you helped me make this book possible.

Sincerely,
Harold Deane Thomason Akins

PART ONE.

THE EARLY YEARS

LOVE AND MARRIAGE

James 2:5. Hearken, my beloved brethren, Hath not God chosen the poor of this world rich in faith, and heirs of the kingdom which he hath promised to them that love him?

Will This Child Fulfill The Dream and Prayer the Father Had For It?

On December 9, 1917, my parents, Mildred Adele Griffin and Harold Deane Thomason were married.

In May 1918, they welcomed the news that a baby was on the way. My mother made a layette for the expected little one and placed in a box the delicate garments that she fashioned so lovingly and beautifully. My father wrote on the cover, "God bless our baby boy and may he grow up to be a fine, Christian man."

My father was the youngest man to join the Masons. He was a member of Landrum Lodge, No. 48, Free and Accepted Masons (F&AM) He was a machinist at the Foundation Company where he was a popular young man.

On December 8, 1918, he died at the age of twenty-three from Spanish influenza and pneumonia during the epidemic that took so many lives. An escort composed of members of the Foundation Company accompanied my father's body to the cemetery.

I arrived January 4, 1919 - just four weeks after my father's death. I am the "son" he expected – hence his name, Harold Deane, was given to me.

One of my father's sisters, who was expecting her first child, died the day I was a week old.

Believe me, I was not born with the proverbial "silver spoon" in my mouth. I was born to a 20-year old widow whose husband had died at an early age. There was no inheritance and just enough insurance for his burial. Nevertheless, "In Jesus my Savior, I am the child of a King."

I also grew up during the "Great Depression" of the 1930s.

My mother went to work soon after I was born, and I was left with my grandparents but still my mother and I spent time together. One day, Mom and I went upstairs in Adler's department store and to my delight, after being cooped up in a small flat, I discovered that only a portion of the large room was being used. This left me a vast area through which I could run round and round at full speed, much to Mom's embarrassment.

The experience at Adler's was not the only time I embarrassed Mom. We were in front of Hogan's department store and I was wearing a beautiful pair of panties with lace and ribbons and bows of which I was very proud, when up walked Mom's gentleman friend Alfred. I immediately pulled up my skirt and showed him Mom's beautiful needlework on my panties.

Mom married again when I was eight years old to Harold Griffith. He and his family had moved to Savannah from Atlanta. Mom and Harold later had two sons, Jack and Fain.

My Grandpapa was a wood-turner, who made beautiful fluted columns, banisters, tables and bowls. I enjoyed watching him work. It amazed me to see him, by himself, take a tree with the bark still on it and use a plank for leverage to move the tree to the lathe or the fluting machine.

During the Great Depression, there was little construction work – just repair work. The family had to go on welfare, and my grandmother took a job as a salad maker at the DeSoto Hotel. That gave me the privilege of swimming in the DeSoto pool.

I believe that was one of the lessons I learned at an early age. There is always a bright side in everything – so look for it.

Another lesson I learned was from Grandpapa who insisted I stick up for myself even if it meant resorting to physical contact. He said he had raised my mother to be too passive and ladylike and he wanted his granddaughter to be able to stand up for herself and not let people take advantage of her or take her possessions away.

I was often sent to my father's sister, Aunt Hattie, to spend the day so I would get a good meal. I always welcomed her heart-felt hugs and kisses.

Aunt Hattie Blanton was the most devout Christian in my family. She – like all Thomasons – was a member of Trinity Methodist Church even though she was married to a Baptist. They went to the churches of their choice on Sunday. Aunt Hattie was involved in the ladies activities at the Trinity Methodist Church where she was a Sunday school teacher. She had a great influence on me when I was growing up. She was a *real* seamstress; she is the one who taught me pattern layout. Her theme was – if something is worth doing at all – it should be done to the best of our ability. She made many of the beautiful dresses I had as a child.

During the growing season, Grandpapa usually had a garden at his shop and we had many wonderful vegetables. I really enjoyed helping him pick the butter beans, and then I raced with him to see who would finish shelling them first. Alas, he always won. My little fingers were not as strong as my desire to beat him.

——— My Father ———

———— Mother and I ————

———— Mom and I Going Shopping ————

My First Trip to the Ocean

Proverbs 20:11a. Even a child makes himself known by his doings.

I was born with a special gene that I call the "Desire to Travel Gene." It is not hereditary. At least I don't think it is. I was the first one in my family to always be ready to go on a trip – if only to the mail box on the corner from our house. If I ever heard anyone say – "I am going to the mail box." I quickly called out, "Wait for me to get my ebby (sweater) so I can go with you."

I also really enjoyed playing in the bath tub. I liked the feel of the water as I splashed it around. Of course, that never pleased my Mother, or my Grandmother, because as I got revved up – water went all over the floor.

In those days there was a train that went to Tybee Island which is on the Atlantic Ocean. I was excited that a big trip was planned for us to go to the beach so I could play in the Big Pond.

My family packed a lunch basket of goodies, and off we went to the train station for our trip.

It was fun to ride on the train again. My first train ride was to LaGrange, Georgia to visit my Grandmother's sister, BUT this ride was more than just a train ride – it was a trip to the ocean.

The family was filled with anticipation and could hardly wait to see my reaction to the ocean. As we walked on the beach toward the water, I started screaming, "Too much 'orter' [water]," and started running full-speed ahead toward the pavilion. My Grandpapa took off in pursuit of the runaway tot. Years later the family told me how disappointed they were at my reaction to the water.

As I grew older, I always enjoyed our Sunday School Picnics at Tybee. There were games for the children, and as we became teenagers, - a Beach Pajama Parade. My dear Aunt Hattie made me some beautiful red pajamas, and I anxiously waited for the parade to start. Thanks to Aunt Hattie's beautiful work, I won the parade that year.

Grandpapa

Aunt Hattie

My illness

Matthew 8:17. That it might be fulfilled which was spoken by Esaias the prophet, saying, Himself took our infirmities, and bare our sicknesses.

God has a way of shaping our lives so that we will become what He wants us to be.

When I was eight years old, I was supposed to be an angel in the Christmas program in our church, but I came down with a bad case of the measles. In early January I developed pneumonia and was put in the hospital. Toward the end of the month I had a double mastoid infection which resulted in an operation. During those critical times a group of ladies at the Epworth Methodist Church, as well as the people in my church, started praying for me.

I recall Mom sitting by my bed many times when I was so sick. During one of these visits she told me that I was going to have a brother or a sister. A few months later my brother Jack was born.

One day my doctor, Dr. G.H. Lange, walked in and told the family there was nothing else he could do for me - that he was leaving the case. He departed with these words, "She is in God's hands." Later he came by and seemed surprised that I was still alive. He said, "She must be left here for a reason." A short time later I was able to return home to Grandpapa and Granny.

I thrived on Grandpapa's praise and advice. He had faith in me. He told me I could do great things if I wanted them bad enough. Sometimes it is good to stretch ourselves. I learned to stretch myself through Grandpapa's encouragement.

One day he turned yo-yos on his lathe and he told me to go sell them. I was a child in elementary school but I did just that. I took a bag of yo-yos to a corner near school and the park and put on a demonstration with a yo-yo.

When I went back home Grandpapa asked me how many I had sold.

I gleefully replied, "Four dozen and fourteen."

Grandpapa then asked, "How many are in one dozen?"

I replied, "Twelve."

"Well then, you sold five dozen and two didn't you?"

That was my first business lesson.

Now I know there were many reasons: my work in the Union Mission, the Bible Clubs, the Mission Youth Camp, Savannah Christian School and, now, my foreign mission work. What a glorious life I have had, and am still having. I don't know why God gave me the privilege of being the cofounder of Savannah Christian School. Many people have rightly said without the Akins, there would be no Savannah Christian Preparatory School today.

Those early years were hard. I don't deny that. Only the Lord knows how I had to juggle the little cash we had in the school bank account to keep the creditors happy. We all worked hard. We cooked for the students on many occasions, cleaned buildings, painted buildings, and cleaned restrooms. We often cared for sick children during the night as all the students lived on campus. I also did a lot of the office work – and taught a class each day.

I went to college, nights and summers, to further my education.

This life could easily have ended at eight years of age, but God spared it for special work He had for her to do in later years. There is much more growing ahead and becoming a vessel fit for God's use.

MY FIRST AIRPLANE RIDE

Isaiah 60:8. "Who are these that fly as a cloud, and as the doves to their windows?"

I was always enthusiastic about airplanes and would dream of being a pilot someday and perhaps even making a parachute jump. I astounded my grandparents with all my wild dreams and desires. I must confess – I never became a pilot- or made a parachute jump; however, my brother and my son became pilots and owned their own planes.

I enjoyed going to the airport and watching planes take off and land. On one occasion, I learned that I could actually go up in a plane for two dollars, but where would I ever get that amount of money for such a wild idea? I started saving for my big adventure with two Indian-head pennies. I also saved my fifteen-cent lunch money by skipping lunch at school until I had the two dollars. My dream was going to come true.

Grandpapa took me out to the airport on August 4, 1934, when I was fifteen years old. We went over to the flying school run by Captain Wilder Enslow and Harold Zinn.

They were quite amazed at my excitement about going up. Mr. Zinn went into his office and brought out his personal cap and goggles and told me to wear them as Capt. Enslow would be taking me through the clouds in an **open cockpit**, two-seater plane. Not many civilians have had the experience of flying in an open cockpit plane. They offered Grandpapa a free ride, which he promptly refused, with this statement, "I'll stay here on terra firma – where there is less terror and more firm."

What a time I had. We did indeed fly through the clouds. I looked down at Savannah and saw the cars going up and down the roads and over the viaducts. They looked like rats running to and fro on a board. I was finally high above earthly things looking down on the city of my birth. I was truly one of the happiest girls in the world. My dream had become a reality. The anticipation was finally realized.

Early in the next school year we were asked to write about our summer vacation and, of course, I wrote about my flight over Savannah with such enthusiasm that my teacher was impressed with my paper, which she took to Mr. Griffith, our Principal, who was writing an English book. I couldn't believe my own ears when He asked me for permission to use my paper in his book.

This was just the beginning of the dreams and ambitions that this young girl would experience as she grew up.

My First Trip to New York –
A Teenager Goes to the Big Apple and on to Marriage

Psalms 34:3. O magnify the Lord with me, and let us exalt his name together.

When I was fifteen years of age, I went to New York with my Grandpapa, who was demonstrating to General Motors executives a gas-saving device that he had invented. I was treated royally by the Carters and the McCartneys.

One of the special privileges I had was signing the same guest book that Amelia Earhart had signed at the Westchester Country Club in Rye, New York. Another privilege that I never had before was to be driven everywhere by a chauffeur.

After seeing many wonderful sites in New York and Brooklyn, and eating in famous restaurants, it was time to head back to Savannah. We arrived back in the Hostess City on Sunday morning in time for me to attend Sunday school.

That morning after the church service, several of the young people approached me about the possibility of going with them that night after church to a youth camp held at Toccoa Falls Bible College. We had all worked hard to raise the money for the trip. As I wasn't expected to be back in time to make the trip with them, my place was given to another girl, who in turn, also had to give up her place. That left a place for me to join them. I didn't have time to pack my suitcase for this trip – I just carried what I had brought home.

Fate was involved – even though I didn't know it at that time. One morning I went to the post office on campus to see if I had any mail from my boy friend back home. There in the post office I met George Akins, who was a student from Savannah attending college there.

I didn't see or hear from George for four years. When I was nineteen years old my Sunday school teacher, Mr. Carl Sack, called me to say he had been invited to conduct an evening service at the Union Mission and wanted me to go along and play the piano for the service.

After the service, I noticed a handsome young man and asked Mr. Sack if he was the George Akins who had attended Toccoa Falls. He said that he didn't know and told me to go ask him. I replied that I couldn't do that, so he called George over to the car. George was indeed the George Akins I had met years before.

I was the hostess of our Sunday School Class, so I immediately invited George to come to Sunday school and church. The next Sunday, he came, and I introduced him to the class. After the class was over, my boy friend said, "Let's go." I replied that I was staying for the church service, so he said that he would pick me up at seven p.m. George stayed for the service, and sat with my Grandmother and me. After the service, he offered us a ride home, which we accepted. When we reached our house, George said that he had to go to Statesboro that afternoon to take his sister and her little girl home. He asked me if I would like to go. I asked my grandmother for permission to go. She said, "Okay," so I told him that I would go with him if he would get me back home in time for my seven o'clock date. He promised he would, and he did.

That was the beginning of a fifty-night steady courtship that ended June 9, 1938, when we were married after an evening service in the Union Mission Chapel, by Rev. J. D. Ibbotson, a visiting evangelist. On the day we had selected, Aunt Hattie and I started out early in the morning to prepare the Mission Chapel for the ceremony. Our first stop was the florist, the second was Trinity Methodist Church where we borrowed two large candelabra and flower baskets.

In lieu of formal wedding attire, I selected a white dress and had a hat with a white veil made to match at Adler's Department Store. The hat was made like George's favorite hat - the black velvet I bought to wear with my fur coat.

Mrs. Woodrow Simms, a coworker at Southern Bell, played the Wedding March for us.

This was the beginning of sixty-one years of marriage and many wonderful experiences together. We had no idea on that June night what lay ahead for us.

Many important things began to happen as we started our journey through life together. We began with love, hope, and a desire to serve the Lord.

MORE EARLY YEARS –
A FEW SMALL ACCOMPLISHMENTS
THAT WERE BIG TO ME

Proverbs 13:19a. The desire accomplished is sweet to the soul...

"What You Are to Be – You Are Now Becoming." Cameron Beck

When in high school, I was taking a course in Journalism. Mr. Cameron Beck, of the New York Stock Exchange, gave a lecture to our class entitled, "What You Are to Be – You Are Now Becoming." Our teacher asked us to write an article for the school newspaper about the lecture. I was thrilled when mine was selected for publication.

In elementary school, I was placed in what was called "The Skipping Class," which meant we would cover two years in one.

Another strong memory from my elementary school years is of my Grandpapa and me. One morning as he was going to Kress' Five and Ten Cent Store, he said. "Come on, Baby, and ride with me." I gleefully ran to the car and jumped in.

When we arrived at the store, he handed me a ten-dollar bill and said, "Spend this on anything you like." I immediately ran to the sewing department in the basement with Grandpapa following a good distance behind. I bought a dress pattern I liked, found a piece of cotton cloth, some thread to match and was determined to make myself a new dress. However, I had a problem, I didn't know how to cut out and sew a garment. After cutting out the garment and sewing it, I discovered I had missed a very important note on the pattern. The back and front both should have been placed on a fold which left the dress with unexpected seams in the middle of the front and middle of the back. Years later, Aunt Hattie taught me pattern layout and sewing.

In junior high, I was one of the ones receiving a school letter.

At Georgia Southern, I was in the Pi Omega Pi – the Honor Society for business education students.

I not only had perfect attendance in Sunday school, I also had perfect attendance for several years in school. In fact, I went all the way through junior high and most of the way through senior high without missing a day. That was quite a record of which I am proud.

I had the privilege of taking elocution lessons from Mrs. Eugene Torrance and was in many plays at the old YWCA Building. I played the part of Dr. Black in one of the plays. Since the doctor was a male, I had to wear a boy's suit. I borrowed one from a neighbor, Frank Durkin, who was about my size. I felt very strange, and was afraid that everyone would laugh at me when I made my appearance on stage. That never happened so all went well that night.

− Me as Dr. Black in a Play at the YWCA −

I started taking piano lessons from Miss Louisa Woeltjen, a teacher who lived a few doors down from us. She had group lessons once a week. My Mother, who was an accomplished musician, had taught me a few things. During one lesson, I wasn't paying attention to Miss Woeltjen, who asked me why I wasn't − so I told her I already knew what she was teaching. She then told me to leave. That was the end of my piano lessons until I went to work and could pay for my lessons. I took lessons for a long time from Mrs. Addie Mae Jackson at Christ Church. The training I received from her was very helpful in later years when I played the piano for the Mission Services, the Mission Youth Camp, and Savannah Christian School.

At this time in my life I did not realize what I would be called on to do in later years.

In my early teens I learned to knit and crochet. I learned these skills by reading books of instruction that publishers sold.

After seeing some pink gloves that I had crocheted to wear with my Easter suit, which I knitted, a young lady in our church asked me to crochet some white ones for her to wear in her June wedding. I was honored to do this for the bride.

As a young girl I had many hobbies. I learned to knit and embroider. In my early years I learned to sew. As an adult, I have always made most of my clothes – including coats and jackets.

Later I did some painting with acrylics. I also joined a ceramics class and made several nice pieces - of which I am very proud.

Our church had a picnic at Tybee each summer. While on the beach, I often looked at the ocean and dreamed of some day crossing the ocean and perhaps, visiting Africa. I have now had that privilege three times - once to Egypt with George, George, Jr. and Barbara. Then I went to Kenya once with no one I had known before the trip, however, my son went with me on my second trip to Nairobi, Kibera, and Kajiado. I am praying that I still may take another trip to Kenya.

As a young child I often played Grandpapa's old victrola with the thick records. I especially liked the one entitled, "On the Beach of Waikiki." I talked to Grandpapa about my desire to see that beach someday. When I went to Hawaii with Doris Hurd, a fellow teacher from South College, as we were swimming there, I looked up to Heaven and said, "Grandpapa, I made it." He had always told me that I could realize my dreams IF I were willing to work hard for them, and believe that it were possible.

I went to Sunday school and church regularly. I had a pin with a wreath and many bars for years of perfect attendance. My teacher, Mr. Carl Sack, often talked to us about articles in Sidney Sheldon's book *What Would Jesus Do?* Mr. Sack encouraged us to always stop and ask that question when in doubt. He also encouraged us to form the habit of praying at noon each day – wherever we were. I started practicing that when Grandpapa and I went to New York with his mechanic, Mr. Batchelor, and GM representative Mr. Koliker. We were going to demonstrate a gas-saving device that Grandpapa had invented. That was quite a trip for the poor little girl from Savannah, Georgia, who had never before been out of this state. Every day as we made our way, I remembered to pray at noon. I especially remember, as we were going through Brooklyn - that I still remembered to pray at noon.

This reminds me of the first night my family and I were in Cairo, as the sun was going down, the Muslims got down on their knees, on the sidewalks, to pray - and what a loud noise they made.

I've learned that whenever I make a decision with an open heart toward the Lord, I usually make the right decision.

An unusual graduation and continuing education

Timothy 2:15. Study to shew thyself approved unto God, a workman that needeth not to be ashamed, rightly dividing the word of truth.

I was like most young people, graduation from high school was very special. It was something we had worked many years to achieve. Our ceremony was held in Savannah, Georgia in 1936 in the auditorium which was later replaced with the Civic Center.

We all felt very proud when we marched to our places on that huge stage, to the tune of "Pomp and Circumstance." We were all dressed in white caps and gowns for the occasion. The girls were to receive their diplomas first, so we all stood up and waited anxiously in line until our names were called. I stood waiting with the girls for my name to be called. As my surname was "Thomason," I was deeply troubled when they started calling names past "T," but my name had not been called. What in the world happened? I completed all the necessary work and had enough credits to graduate. How I wished the floor would open up at that very moment and rescue me from this awkward situation.

We all sat down and the young men stood up waiting for their names to be called. You guessed it. My name was called right along with the boys, and I had to march around to the front of the stage in front of everybody to receive my diploma while everyone laughed and clapped. That was one of the times in my life I wished that my name was "Mary," or any other feminine name rather than having been named "Harold Deane" for my father.

My next step up the education ladder was the Draughon Business College in Savannah. This was my first college graduation. It was another milestone, but rather uneventful.

An AAB degree from Armstrong State College, also in Savannah, came next. It was only a two-year college, but another step toward my goal of achieving a Master of Education (MED) in School Administration.

On to Georgia Southern where I attended classes for the next three years.

Commuting to Statesboro in those days meant traveling Highway 80 through Pooler and Bloomingdale in Georgia, and other small towns. As soon as I finished my Bachelor in Science (BS) degree in Business Education, the interstate highway, I-16, was completed. This made traveling to school easier.

I had the privilege of attending Wheaton College in Illinois for one summer. Attending the Chapel services there was one of the greatest blessings I had along the way to reaching my goal. I was there about the time the missionaries were killed in South America. They had a strong tie to Wheaton as several of the missionaries had attended school there.

I later had one summer at Middle College of Georgia, and several correspondence courses.

There were still many things to accomplish, and I have never tired of studying and learning.

Proof That I Did Receive a Diploma

MY FIRST JOB AND FIRST VACATION

2 Thessalonians 3:10. For even when we were with you, this we commanded you, that if any would not work, neither should he eat.

After graduation from high school, I desperately wanted to go on to college, however, there was no money, so I started looking for a job. I found one the first place I applied. I was very happy when I went home and told my grandparents that I had been hired by Southern Bell to go in for training to become a long-distance operator.

After my training I began working full-time and received a weekly check. After a deduction of ten cents for Social Security, I received a check in the amount of $9.90. It was amazing how much could be bought with that small amount of money. One special item that I bought from Fine's Department Store was a silver fox fur coat. I also bought a black velvet dress and hat that completed my Christmas attire.

Mr. Leroy Suddath was the district traffic manager of Southern Bell and had an office in our building. He was always very nice to me and encouraged and challenged me to do my best for Southern Bell.

When they needed an operator to check the line finders that showed traffic flow on the phone lines, I was the one called on to do the job. I worked hard, because I knew he believed in me.

When he heard that I was planning to get married, he called for me to come to his office. When I arrived there, he wished me much happiness and told me that he had some very good advice for me. I told him that I always welcomed good advice. This is what he told me, "Always agree with your husband, and then do whatever you please." I have always followed his advice.

My fellow workers gave me a set of china at my shower that I loved dearly and used for many years.

Many of the young people from our church were going to the Cincinnati Bible College. My friends asked me to ride the train with them to Cincinnati and spend a week sightseeing in the big city, which I did as I had been working for a good while and was entitled to a vacation. I planned to go with them.

The young people who were making the trip gathered with their families and Grandpa and me at the train station to wait for the call, "All aboard." After much hugging, kissing, and bidding "*Adieu,*" we boarded the "Iron Horse" for our long ride to Ohio.

I really enjoyed my trip up with my friends and had a wonderful time while I was there. We frequented Stone's Chili Pot, a favorite eating place for the students. I saw real snow on the ground for the first time in my life. We rode the incline railway and went to a radio station to see a dramatic group put on a play on the air. We even took a short ride over the state line – just for the fun of it. We also skated at the famous Zefferino Roller Dome.

My return trip – all alone - was not much fun. We went up by train, but I returned by bus, which seemed to be an endless ride.

MY NEW BIRTH –
A BIG STEP THAT WOULD CHART MY LIFE

Romans 10:9. "That if thou shalt confess with thy mouth the Lord Jesus, and shalt believe in thine heart that God hath raised him from the dead, thou shalt be saved."

Romans 10:13. For whosoever shall call upon the name of the Lord shall be saved.

I was christened in the Trinity Methodist Church, the church that my father's family attended.

We later moved to the Southside and started attending the neighborhood church – The Central Church of Christ. I was enrolled in the Cradle Roll Class at a very early age, and continued in that church until after I married George and joined him in attending the Independent Presbyterian Church.

While growing up, I attended regularly and received a pin with many bars.

When I was in my early teens, we had a revival meeting and I went forward when the invitation was given to join the church. That is exactly what I did – I joined the church. I was baptized shortly thereafter.

In later years, I was in a service where the preacher asked the question, "If you died in that seat, where you are sitting right now, are you sure that you have been born again and are on your way to heaven?" I had never heard preaching like that. No, I was not sure that I had been born again and I couldn't be sure I would be in heaven if I died right there.

I went home quite troubled. I wanted to go to Heaven and evidently I needed to be born again. I went into my bedroom, got down on my knees and poured out my heart to the Lord. I asked Him to forgive me for my sins, those of omission, as well as those of commission, to save me, and give me the assurance that I had been born again. I can truthfully say that since that night so many years ago, I have had the assurance that I am on my way to Heaven. Not because of any good works that I might have done, but because Jesus had paid for my sins on the Cross of Calvary. I felt like a tremendous burden had been lifted, and had been replaced with joy and happiness. I didn't want to ever lose the joy and happiness that I had that night.

Paul tells us in the first of the prison books "For by grace are ye saved through faith; and that not of yourselves: It is the gift of God: Not of works, lest any man should boast." (Ephesians 2:8-9)

I now wanted to live for Him and to help spread the Good News of Salvation, wherever the Lord led me. My prayer is that I will be clay in His Mighty Hands, and that He will continue to cut off the rough edges and make me a vessel that He can use to bring the lost to a saving knowledge of Jesus Christ.

Part two

Planting and reaping

Union mission, inc.

Luke 15:7. I say unto you, that likewise joy shall be in heaven over one sinner that repenteth, more than over ninety and nine just persons, which need no repentance.

One night, my future husband George Akins was riding on a bus from Atlanta to Toccoa, Georgia, which is located approximately 90 miles northeast of Atlanta. He was asleep when the bus came to a sudden stop. There had been an awful accident and two young men were lying on the highway apparently dead. George thought that if there had been a place somewhere along the way where they could have gotten a night's lodging they probably would not be there in that condition.

Right there, that dark night, the Union Mission of Savannah, was born in George's heart.

Soon after that George returned to Statesboro, Georgia. He was very ill with Brill's Fever. After a long illness, he was ready to begin work on his dream of a home for the homeless.

He came to Savannah, got a job and a place to live. He began talking to people about the proposed project. One person with a listening ear was his Pastor, Dr. Samuel Glasgow.

He had served as George's mentor since his conversion in the Independent Presbyterian Church.

After much work, and many disappointments along the way, the Union Rescue Mission opened at 416 West Liberty Street in a former drug store on April 20, 1937. (That took place before my time at the mission. I joined George in the work in 1938 after our wedding.)

Two special men were present that night, Dr. Glasgow and Charles Huston from Coatesville, Pa. After the service, Mr. Huston told George that he liked the spirit of the meeting. Thus began years of continued gifts to the Mission and to George and me from the Hustons. Every Christmas two red envelopes came with checks in them - one for the Mission and one for the Akins.

The Mission began giving food and shelter to the homeless. Evening services were held with George, a local minister or layman giving a gospel message and an invitation to accept the Lord Jesus Christ. A Sunday school was soon added and then Bible Clubs for children.

Sometime after its beginning, George and I noticed a large "For Sale" sign posted on a three-story brick building across the street. The price - $12,500. George and I immediately started praying for that building. We got a key and walked through it - claiming it for the Lord. We wondered how the layout was just what we would need for a larger work for the Lord.

One day George and Dr. Newell Turner were walking together downtown. The doctor asked George if we were still praying for the building. George replied that we were indeed still praying for that building. Dr. Turner told George that he would give $2,500 toward the purchase price, and would lend him the balance.

Many years after moving into the building at 415 West Liberty Street, with a lovely chapel given by Miss Mary Clay in honor of her brother Thomas Savage Clay, who was interested in Mission work in New York, a Mr. Hurley, from New York attended a chapel service. After the service, he told George and me that he had preached in that building many years before. We doubted that right away because we knew it had housed a bank and an auto agency, but never a religious institution; however the next week, out of curiosity, we decided to check out his statement.

We found a listing in an old city directory of a rescue mission at that address, just as Mr. Hurley had said. Later we uncovered the following fact from documents found in the cornerstone of the building, *"This building was built in 1888 by the Women's Christian Temperance Union For a Mission."* After a few years it closed and we moved into it in 1940, not knowing its history.

Another very amazing part of this story is, George opened his Mission across the street exactly 49 years, less one day, after the original one had opened across the street. No wonder the new home of the Mission appeared to us to have been built to our exact needs.

God's wonders never cease.

The Mission operated in the building until Urban Development claimed the property for the construction of a new area for the Civic Center.

When George retired, the new superintendent and his board, changed the name to the "Grace House" and also changed the program to a social one.

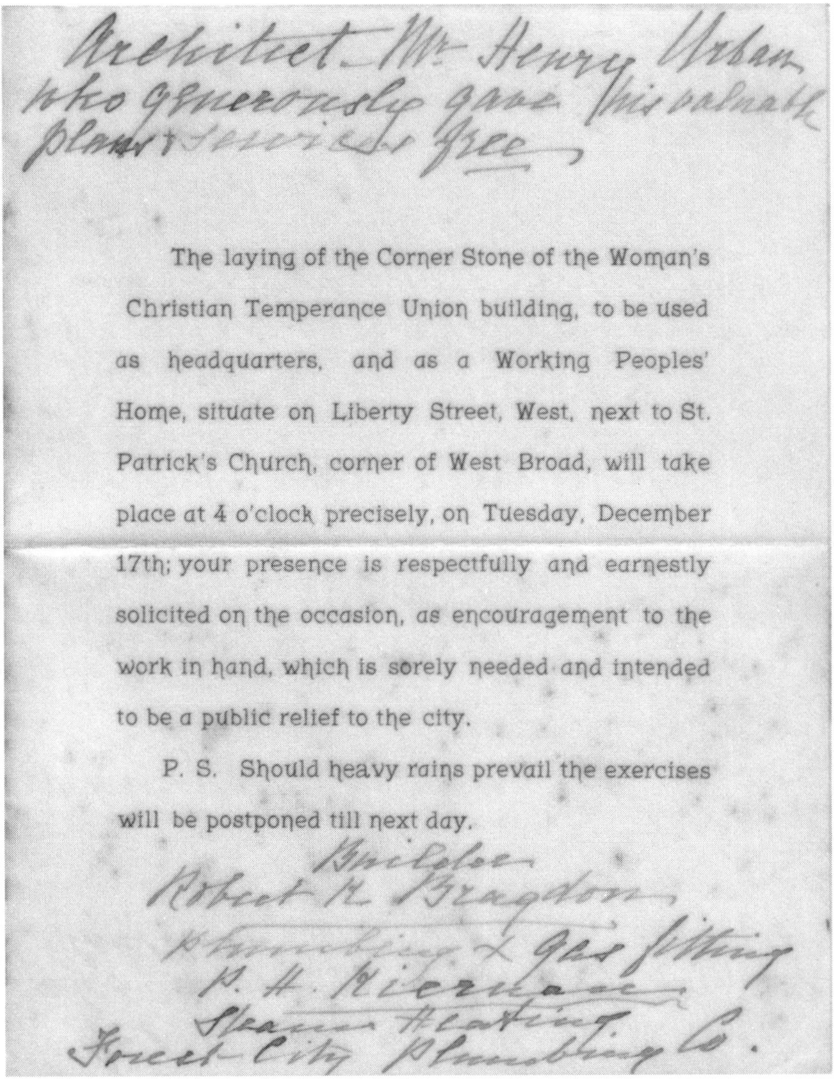

Architect. Mr. Henry Urban, who generously gave this valuable plans & services free

The laying of the Corner Stone of the Woman's Christian Temperance Union building, to be used as headquarters, and as a Working Peoples' Home, situate on Liberty Street, West, next to St. Patrick's Church, corner of West Broad, will take place at 4 o'clock precisely, on Tuesday, December 17th; your presence is respectfully and earnestly solicited on the occasion, as encouragement to the work in hand, which is sorely needed and intended to be a public relief to the city.

P. S. Should heavy rains prevail the exercises will be postponed till next day.

*Builder
Robert R. Bragdon
Plumbing & gas fitting
P. H. Kiernan
Steam heating
Forest City Plumbing Co.*

———— Document Found in the Cornerstone of the ————
Original Rescue Mission When It Was Razed

Petition for Incorporation

State of Georgia.
Chatham County.

The petition of Mrs Mary A. Webb, Mrs Martha S. Inglesby, Miss Paula Harris, Mrs J. W. Henderson, Mrs Eliza Feddis, Mrs Adline Harrison, Mrs Catharine Rutherford, Mrs Mary Beckett, Miss Martha Lindsay, Miss Willie Swoll, Miss Louise Marguerite Harriman, Mrs Clara M. Ellis, and others, all of said County and State, respectfully show that they desire to be incorporated under the corporate name of "The Woman's Christian Temperance Union of Savannah, Georgia," that their association is for educational, charitable, social and religious purposes; that they are about to establish, in connection therewith, halls, schools, and reading rooms in said County, for the purpose of disseminating the principles of Christian Temperance.

Petition for Incorporation for the Original Rescue Mission at 415 W. Liberty Street, Savannah, Which Later Housed Our Rescue Mission

Endorsement.

In Chatham Superior Court.

In Re:—

Petition of "The Woman's Christian Temperance Union of Savannah, Georgia," for Incorporation.
Order of Incorporation, filed in office and recorded this 19th day of April, 1888.   James K. P. Carr

Clerk S. C. C. C.

(Mer No. 49 fol. 167.)

A. H. Mac Donell, atty for Petitioners

Order of Court granting incorporation filed in my office & entered in Minutes of Chatham Superior Court.
19th day of April A. D. 1888.   James K. P. Carr

Clerk S. C. C. C. Geo.   H. F.

Additional Court Document Pertaining to the
Incorporation of the Original Rescue Mission

I JOINED GEORGE IN THE WORK
OF THE UNION MISSION

Romans 8:28. And we know that all things work together for good to them that love God, to them who are the called according to His purpose.

After George and I were married and had a short honeymoon to St. Augustine, Florida, I joined in the work of the Union Mission. On Sunday afternoons, I taught a Sunday School Class there. I also played the piano for both services – afternoons and evenings. I joined the Independent Presbyterian Church, where George had accepted the Lord at the age of 26. George and I attended Sunday School and Church in the mornings. In later years, George, Jr. went with us.

I continued working at the Savannah Fire Department Headquarters on Oglethorpe Avenue. This was during World War II, so the three ladies who each worked an eight-hour shift, were under strict rules and regulations. Headquarters was truly the central point of all fire activities in Savannah. Our switchboard must be protected. We were, therefore, locked in our office with black curtains, and a pistol to protect the equipment, and us, if needed. When our station went out on calls at night, they left all the garage doors open downstairs. We were told not to open our office door during these times.

One morning after completing the midnight shift, I went home to the Union Mission. As I walked into the hall, the phone rang and half-asleep I answered, "Fire Department." The caller quickly said, "Wrong number," and hung up.

When the war ended, so did our jobs.

A new work came right along – Children's Bible Club work.

INTERNATIONAL UNION OF GOSPEL MISSIONS

Psalms 103:5. Who satisfieth thy mouth with good things; so that thy youth is renewed like the eagle's.
[This verse always reminds me of Ma Sunday.]

George and I were members of the International Union of Gospel Missions for many years, consequently we had the privilege of attending a convention sponsored by one of the missions in the "Union" each year, usually during the month of May. Some of the outstanding Christian men in the United States were superintendents of rescue missions.

Attending those conventions and hearing the testimonies of men like Harry Saulnier of the Pacific Garden Mission in Chicago; Pat Withrow of the Gospel Rescue Mission in Charleston, West Virginia; and Rev. George Bolton of the Bowery Mission in New York City were some of the experiences that helped shape my life.

Mrs. Billy Sunday was one of the keynote speakers for many years. When we hosted the convention here in Savannah, "Ma," as she was called, spent some time with me at the mission. One day we walked up the steps to the powder room on the second floor. When we reached the top step, Ma turned quickly around and asked me how many steps were there. She was quite surprised that I didn't know. She said that she never walked up steps without counting them.

Ma told us on the night that Billy died she asked God why didn't He take her instead of Billy, as Billy was far more useful to the Lord's work than she was; however, she said before the night was over, she promised the Lord that she would be willing to do anything that He asked her to do. A few days later she received a phone call asking her to preach the funeral of a friend. She questioned whether she could do that since Billy's loss was so great and so recent. She made the decision to preach the funeral. She was truly one of the greatest women I have ever met. How I wish I could be more like her.

I must tell you about our airplane flight to the convention in Grand Rapids, MI. We arrived safely in Kokomo, Indiana. We had a delay there as they had announced there was a problem with our plane which they were repairing. While sitting there, George told me to go change our flight to the next flight because he didn't want to go on that plane. I did as he requested. We were left sitting at the airport for several hours, and would also miss the opening banquet, which was always the highlight of the conventions.

When we were finally airborne, I looked out at the number on the wing of the plane, and would you believe – we were on the same plane. We had waited at the airport while it went to Chicago and returned to Kokomo for another load. I definitely was not a happy camper that evening when we arrived in Grand Rapids hours after everything was over.

GEORGE, JR. ARRIVES

Psalms 127:3. *"Lo, children are an heritage of the Lord:*
and the fruit of the womb is his reward."

When George and I were married, we were hoping to have a baseball team of sons. We were having our devotions one evening and read that verse from the Psalms. We got down on our knees and asked the Lord to give us a son. We prayed that prayer before he was conceived. When we told our doctor that story, he said that George, Jr. had a heritage that very few children have. However, our dream of a team was not to be.

On February 13, 1940, our only son arrived at the Candler Hospital. What a happy day that was for us, because our son arrived safely after an anxious time. He weighed 8 lbs. 12 oz. at birth and had lots of black hair. He had such beautiful, tiny hands. When I saw him for the first time he held onto my hand. I don't think a child was ever born who was loved more than he was. He was our pride and joy. Of course we thought that he was the most handsome and the smartest child in the whole world.

Just before George Jr. and I left the hospital, Dr Everett Iseman came by to see me before checking us out. We asked him how much we owed him for the Caesarean Section delivery. Dr. Iseman handed me $2.00 and told me his fee was as follows – We were to open a bank account for George, Jr. and add two dollars to it each week, so he would be able to go to college.

That dear old Jewish doctor used to come to see us when we lived upstairs in the Union Mission. He never charged us for any of his visits or our visits to his office. For years we prayed for him, and with him. He was very special to us.

George, Jr. was christened at Independent Presbyterian Church by Dr. Samuel M. Glasgow, and attended Sunday school and church with us.

Mr. E.N. Upshaw, the president of the Union Mission and an official of Prudential Life Insurance Company, invited George, George, Jr., and me to accompany him on his business trip to Statesboro. While in route, Mr. Upshaw told us he realized that because we were doing the

Lord's work we would not have a large financial inheritance to leave our son. Therefore, he urged us to make certain George, Jr. received a good education so he could take care of himself. We took his advice to heart and educated George, Jr. to the best of our financial ability.

When he was enrolled in a kindergarten class at the Trinity Methodist Church during the war, many of the parents of the children in his class were working in the local shipyards. Most were making more money than ever before. One day the teacher was talking with the children and as each child told about the big salaries their parents were making, George, Jr. listened and when she got to him he said, "My parents don't have so much money, but I guess they have enough."

One beautiful day when George, Jr. was young, he and his Dad were walking across one of the fields on the school grounds. Little George looked up toward Heaven and said, "Dad, Jesus is not coming back today." His Dad asked, "Why?" George, Jr. replied, "Because the Bible says 'Behold, He cometh with clouds and there is not a cloud in the sky.'" That statement shows the importance of teaching children God's Word. Even though he was quite young at that time, he remembered the scripture and was able to connect that statement with current skies.

We had a farm on the Telfair Road where George supervised men from the Union Mission who worked out there. When the watermelons were ripe, they brought a load to the Mission and George was planning to sell them on the sidewalk. George, Jr. stepped up and asked his Dad if he could sell some for him. He was told to sell them for $1.00. Things were going along very well, until a man came up and asked him to cut one in half and sell it to him for fifty cents. George, Jr. told him he could cut it any way he wanted to - the price was still $1.00.

About a year later we were riding a train to New York where George was to conduct a revival meeting. He had been giving out gospel tracts – as there were a lot of soldiers on the train. George. Jr. asked his Dad if he could give out some. He took a few and went down the aisle to give them out. One soldier gave him fifty cents. He came running back and asked his Dad for more tracts.

George attended Pape School for his first five years. The school was started by Miss Nina Pape, a member of the Independent Presbyterian Church. Many of the teachers were also members of our church. George, Jr. left when we learned there would be no boys in his sixth grade class, but there would be eleven girls. We knew that wouldn't be a good situation for him. We hated to give up the good educational program, but it seemed necessary to us. He was so far ahead of the pupils academically in the new school that he played for about three years. His teachers kept telling me they couldn't keep him busy. He would finish his work quickly and then wanted to play. When we started a junior high section at Savannah Christian School he came to our school. He was in the Spanish class that I was teaching, and he said that I was the hardest teacher he ever had.

When a teenager, George, Jr. was a counselor at the Mission Youth Camp during the summer. He had a group of young boys in Cabin 1. We were very proud of the job he did.

He joined a baseball league and became an outstanding pitcher. He pitched one no-hitter, and had a bag full of balls, one for each game he had won.

He went to Presbyterian College for two years on a baseball scholarship, then went to work and finally finished at Georgia Southern, where he graduated with honors.

George, Jr. worked for Bernhardt Industries in Lenoir, North Carolina, where he was vice president in charge of sales. They had him upgrade his pilot's license to an instrument rating instead of a visual one because he piloted their plane all over the United States. When he left that company, he bought another plane and flew George, Sr. and me on many trips.

He is married to Barbara Sharon Kicklighter and they have two daughters and five grandchildren.

George owns and operates his own sales agency which acts as factory representatives for large furniture factories. He employs several sales reps who cover Georgia, Florida, Alabama, and the Caribbean Islands.

George and his family live in Boca Raton, Florida.

BARBARA AKINS (MRS. GEORGE, JR.)

I cannot leave this section without mentioning my daughter-in law. No mother ever had a more wonderful one than I have. She has been a wonderful help-mate to my son. I am so glad that she is the mother of my grandchildren.

She has been like a daughter to me and I love her dearly.

George, Jr.

Five Generations: George Jr.'s Two Daughters and
Their Two Sons, George, Jr., My Mother, and Me

MISSION YOUTH CAMP

Proverbs 22:6. "Train up a child in the way that he should go, and when he is old, he will not depart from it."

After having Bible Clubs every afternoon in different parts of the city for several years, ending with a big Vacation Bible School at the Union Mission on Liberty Street during the summer, God laid on our hearts the Mission Youth Camp which opened in 1947.

The camp consisted of twelve cabins, three shower houses, and a dining hall which were built on Telfair Road in Savannah. Later a big, open-air tabernacle and a swimming pool were added.

At the board meeting when the proposed camp was discussed and suggested names were brought up, Edgar Eyler came up with the name that was chosen, which was "Mission Youth Camp."

At first, boys and girls who came regularly to the Bible clubs and memorized Bible verses, were treated to a free week at camp. A large group was eligible to go out there the first summer, but alas, there was no electricity. The power company had to run a line from the Louisville Road to the camp, and they were behind schedule. With George and me a promise to children must be kept – even against all odds.

A truckload of boys and girls was brought out on schedule, as promised, and oil lamps were placed in each cabin. All the cooking was done in our house. They used our bathroom, and spread out on the floor of our living room and dining room for Bible classes. I believe we would all say – that was the best camp ever.

Later scholarships of $10 per child were raised in order to be able to give more children the benefit of a week out of the hot city at camp where they could enjoy a real vacation. We averaged 100 boys and girls each week for the entire summer.

Each morning began with breakfast in the dining hall. There were ten tables with ten children and a counselor at each table. There was singing of choruses and a Bible verse for the day was given.

After breakfast, we all gathered around the flag pole where pledges were recited to the American flag, the Christian flag, and the Bible.

Then came campus and cabin clean-up time. Beds were made, cabins swept, and shower houses cleaned.

At 10 a.m. all the children went to an assigned class with a teacher where a visual Bible lesson was usually given. Bible verses were assigned to be memorized before the next class session.

At high noon the bell rang and everyone went to the dining hall for lunch. Once again there was singing and George often told a little joke which everyone enjoyed, especially the children. They laughed hilariously at every joke. One day he ran out of jokes so made up one that made no sense at all, but he knew he could count on the children laughing. This is what he said, "One day I was driving down the street and I met a car. We passed each other and continued on our way." Then the usual laughter followed. The next day one of the dear counselors told him that she still didn't understand his joke. Different tables sang verses of songs, and everyone had a good time.

The time of day that the staff enjoyed, but the children didn't – was quiet time. To the boys and girls that hour was the longest hour of the day because the pool was in the center of the cabins and they all wanted to *dive in*.

After swimming, shower time was next on the agenda. Then the evening meal, boating, and fishing.

Chapel time in the evening was the last time each day that we were all together. Several different types of evening services were enjoyed. The camp fire night was one of the favorites. There testimonies were often given by the staff and the children. Then they roasted marshmallows.

What a joy it was to see boys and girls give their hearts to the Lord. One evening service stands out in my memory. It was July 10, 1948. That night Anne Tyson, John Davis, Harry Morris, and Bill Reagan all accepted the Lord as their personal Savior. They all became outstanding Christians. John died in a helicopter crash while in the Service. Bill became a minister, Anne a teacher, and Harry a music director in his church.

Saturday morning the campers packed up and headed back to town on the bus. Those of us who were left behind had the pleasant job of cleaning the camp as a church group usually came out for a picnic in the afternoons. Gertrude Smith and I were always especially blessed - we had the pleasure of cleaning the shower houses. After one hundred children had used them for the week with no heavy cleaning, and some of the children had never learned what that little handle on the toilet was for, it was a pretty mess. Gertrude and I had to make a joke of it in order to make it through a cleaning. We called ourselves the 5 C's - the Certified Chatham County Commode Cleaners. That made the job so much easier.

I look back on those summers as the happiest of my life. Only eternity will reveal the lives that were changed because of the Mission Youth Camp. One of the members of my Sunday School Class says he found the Lord at the camp. One young lady, Linda Stegall, who lived in Jacksonville, came to visit some of her family here in Savannah, and came to the camp with them. She is now a full-time Missionary in Kiev, Ukraine. Our own Independent Presbyterian Church is currently helping to support her and her work. Margaret Holton, one of our graduates, married John Stauffacher a fine young missionary and they have spent their lives in France as missionaries.

I often still meet men and women at different places who say, "I went to the Mission Youth Camp and found a new life in Christ."

That statement brings to me more joy than all the riches of the world.

Our Secretary Who Prayed
With Us About School

Mission Youth Club No. 1 - Bingville

Mission Youth Club No. 4 - Bona Bella

Mission Youth Club No. 2 - Union Mission

——————— Evelyn Roberts and Campers ———————

——————— Mary Edna Rex and Campers ———————

Missionary Florence Bradley
and Her Campers

"Happy" Kitchen Crew Kept the
Dishes and Dining Hall Spotless

Mission Youth Camp Cabins

Children In Front Of Cabin

A Buggy Ride

Campers At Play

Mission Lake

Dining Room

Studying God's Word

BEGINNING OF THE EVANGELICAL BIBLE INSTITUTE, NOW SAVANNAH CHRISTIAN PREPARATORY SCHOOL

Matthew 7:24. Therefore whosoever heareth these sayings of mine, and doeth them, I will liken him unto a wise man, which built his house upon a rock.

George had attended Toccoa Falls Bible College as a student, and I met him there while attending a summer camp. We were both deeply impressed with Dr. R. A. Forrest, the teachers, and the students we met at that college. It was clearly different than any school I had ever attended. Years later the Evangelical Bible Institute was born in the Akins' hearts. You may ask why? In those days, there were no private Christian schools in Chatham County. We were the pioneers. and had planned to add a Bible Institute later on. The other day I came across some papers that George had written a long time ago. One was entitled – "The Purpose of Savannah Christian School." He pointed out the two main purposes:

1. To bring as many young people as possible to a saving knowledge of our Lord and Savior Jesus Christ.

2. To help them grow in grace and the knowledge of Jesus Christ.

At that time the slogans were

- Where the Bible Comes First.
- Where Character is Developed with Intellect.
- Teach Young People How To Live, As Well As How To Make A Living.

My prayer is that – the original purpose will never be forgotten. I am so thankful that I had the privilege of being the cofounder of this school with George, which reminds me of I Cor: 3:6 where the Apostle Paul said that he planted, Apollos watered, but God gave the increase. George and I planted and many people have watered, but God has given the increase. To Him Be the Glory.

I want to call your attention to the following verses:

I Cor. 3:6-11. *I have planted, Apollos watered; but God gave the increase. So then neither is he that planteth any thing, neither he that watereth; but God that giveth the increase. Now he that planteth and he that watereth are one; and every man shall receive his own reward according to his own labour. For we are labourers together with God: ye are God's husbandry, ye are God's building. According to the grace of God which is given unto me, as a wise masterbuilder, I have laid the foundation, and another buildeth thereon. But let every man take heed how he buildeth thereupon. For other foundation can no man lay than that is laid, which is Jesus Christ.*

Also, in Matthew 7 and Luke 9 we read the account of wise men who built their houses on a rock. THIS SCHOOL WAS FOUNDED ON THE ROCK — JESUS CHRIST. I firmly believe that if the Lord doesn't return for his church in the next 50 years - this school will be here for its one hundredth anniversary.

During the summer camp session of 1950 after the meals, George and I, along with some of the counselors, would go to a table in the corner of the dining hall and have special prayer concerning our desire to start a Christian school in the City of Savannah. After camp was over, George, our office secretary, and I continued to pray that we may know God's Will in this important matter.

The year 1951 began with the three of us again on our knees in the office praying about our dream. We decided to do what Gideon had done – put out a fleece. Our fleece was this – we asked God to give us His Seal of Approval to go ahead with the school by giving us $10,000 during the month of January. We knew that it was a tremendous undertaking, but we also knew that if God were leading, it would be successful.

After our prayer meeting that morning, George went to the home of Dr. and Mrs. Newell Turner. He told them of our strong desire to start a Christian school here in Savannah, and asked them for $1,000. They surprised him by saying that they had been praying for such a school in Savannah for many years. They gave the first gift – not $1,000, but $2,500. The dear old doctor teased George for not asking them for more than $1,000 and often jokingly called him of little faith.

I do not recall the names of all who contributed toward the goal we had set, but George and I gave one of the $1,000 gifts. I wish I could recall each of them for they had such an important part in the beginning of our school. Only Eternity will reveal the importance of their gifts toward the establishment of this school.

Let me remind you that money was not as plentiful in those days as it is today. Let's move forward to January 31, 1951. We had $8,500 and it was now around 4 o'clock and we were once again on our knees in the office of the Union Mission when the phone rang. George reached over and picked up the phone. It was Waldo Bradley of the Bradley Plywood Company. Mr. Bradley said, "George, sometime ago you invited me to go with you to see the proposed site of a school. I have a little time this afternoon, if it is convenient for you." *Why this afternoon?* Was it convenient? Of course it was.

George picked him up and they rode out to the Mission Youth Camp on the Telfair Road. After riding around the grounds, they stopped in front of the open-air tabernacle where George told him what we were praying about.

George took Mr. Bradley back to his office. After he got out of the car, he walked around to George's side of the car and said, "Put me down for $1,500.00." What if he had not called —or had not made the contribution—would there be a Savannah Christian School today?

The dream of a Christian School here in Savannah, which was born in the Akins' hearts, started to become a reality.

Then the real work began - remodeling the summer camp buildings so that they could be used for the school until permanent buildings could be constructed.

I learned a few new skills during those months - how to put up sheet rock and how to tape it, how to paint, how to put down tile, and as summer approached - how to work in nearly 100-degree temperature without air-conditioning. I didn't realize that I was being prepared for my later work in Kenya and Haiti.

Not only were we working on buildings, we were also planning a curriculum, ordering textbooks, hiring teachers, and performing many other tasks that go along with a school. Since the students would be living on campus, there would be meals to prepare, menus to be planned, and groceries to be ordered.

We had set September 17, 1951, as the opening date. That was one date that wasn't slow in coming. We worked long, hard hours to have everything ready, but thank the Lord, we reached our goal.

We began that year with two full-time teachers, two part-time ones, and George and me.

We started with eight high school students, four boys and four girls. The boys were Buddy Hall, Thomas Harrelson, Joseph Latimer, and Bill Reagan. The girls were Anne Tyson, Barbara Futch, Gene Porter, and Mary Ann Zealy. In January, two more students entered – Millie Farlow and Ronald Shaw.

Mary Edna Rex and Ardell Jacquot were our two full-time teachers. They lived on the campus and were in charge of the students – which included conducting a study hall session each evening. Later Gertrude Smith was in charge of the girls' dorm and Jack Jackson was our cook.

Our part-time teachers were Rev. and Mrs. Ralph Godwin who taught the Bible classes, served as substitutes, and helped out with counseling.

Each morning began with a chapel service which George usually conducted, or a local minister. Chapel was followed by a gathering around the flag-pole where pledges were made to the American flag, the Christian flag, and the Bible.

I served as principal for the first two years until Miss Anna Clarke was hired as principal and math teacher. By the time she retired, I had completed my Masters in Education at Georgia Southern and once again became principal. My job description was far more complex than an ordinary principal. I planned the curriculum and selected the textbooks, hired the teachers, planned the menus, ordered the groceries, checked and paid the bills, was secretary to the board, and had to do many menial jobs. Since we had many boarding students, some from foreign countries, I was often called during the night to check on a sick student. I even had to admit a couple to the hospital during the wee hours.

I often worked 24/7 and all without a salary for over twenty-two years. I finally received a salary of $400.00 per month as a fully certified principal. It might not have been a great amount materially but the joy of seeing the school grow and young people being dedicated to the Lord cannot be measured in dollars and cents.

My husband, who was the President of the school and also the Superintendent of the Union Mission, along with the Board members, raised the money for buildings, but they left the curriculum, and day by day activities up to me and my faculty. I served as secretary to the Board and handled all the finances of the school with the approval of the Board. This procedure was followed all the years we were there. Our records were audited by an accountant every year from 1951 on.

I especially remember one chapel service when the power of God came down and nearly everyone present was weeping before the Lord and asking His forgiveness - and that of other students and faculty they felt they had wronged. That chapel service lasted nearly three hours and was one of the highlight experiences of my life and that of many present that morning. This mountain-top experience was followed by 24-hour prayer meetings. Someone was on their knees every hour, day and night in what was then an open-air tabernacle. Students, faculty, and parents all joined in prayer for our school.

One of the special experiences of those early years were days of fasting. How I thank the Lord for those wonderful days. Not many Christians have experienced that joy.

While the school was in its early stage, we were able to do many things that were not possible as the school grew. One was the fun the seniors had each year on Sadie Hawkins Day, a Senior Sneak Day. On the day that was selected and guarded tenaciously, the seniors and I rushed out and took off for a day of fun at the Ogeechee River. George went ahead and took our boat, and I had loaded up our picnic lunch. All students had a try at water skiing. I wish I had a movie of that event it was so hilarious.

Several times we chartered nine busses and left in the wee morning hours for a day at Disney World in Orlando. Each bus had teachers or parents as chaperones. On one trip it rained all day, nevertheless, we had much fun.

I also had the privilege of chaperoning senior trips to New York which bring back many happy memories.

Our school always had a chorus, a trio, and a quartet that went to sing in different churches throughout this area. We had several excellent soloists.

Barbara Kicklighter, now our daughter-in-law, went with George and me to an International Union of Gospel Missions Convention. Barbara sang a solo for the whole group in Minneapolis.

Every student attended chapel at least two times per week and took a course in the Bible every year.

Those were truly the "Glory Years" of Savannah Christian, and I thank the Lord I had the wonderful privilege of being a part of them.

During those years George was teaching a Bible Class – first at Independent Presbyterian Church and then at Bull Street Baptist Church.

Several of the students and I started a Sunday school in Deptford Homes in East Savannah. The school drew a large group of adults, young people, and children. We continued that program until Riverside Baptist Church opened and provided a Sunday school.

The students, George and I also had old-fashioned street meetings on Bull and Broughton Streets on Saturdays. We would drive our little station wagon down to the corner, let the tail-gate down, climb up and give our testimonies.

In later years, I also taught a Sunday school class of teen-agers at the Independent Presbyterian Church.

As I look back over these 50 years, there is a sad note – some of the students who were in that first class in 1951 and have walked on these sacred grounds have passed away.

Anne Tyson, our first graduate, went on to Bob Jones University where she graduated and went to California to teach children. She became a reading specialist and received many National Honors for her accomplishments. She returned to Savannah Christian for the Fiftieth Graduation Ceremony.

While principal, I set up the Open Court Reading Program for the elementary students. It was based on a phonetic system. It was a great success as I proved by testing the first graders on the same spelling list as the ninth graders. The first graders scored higher overall results – because the older students had been taught the sight system. They could not sound out a new word.

When I visited some schools in Guatemala, I was especially impressed with the fact that they all wore uniforms. Was that the reason they were so well disciplined? Could wearing a uniform give you pride in your school and the fact that you were a part of the school. I was told by some of the teachers that students did indeed behave much better when dressed in uniforms.

When I returned I began planning to select attractive uniforms for our students. Our school colors were red and white, "red for the blood of Christ, and white for His Purity", hence those colors were incorporated in the colors chosen. We selected red blazers with white school emblems. The girls wore plaid skirts and white blouses. The boys wore white shirts and dress pants.

I started the Internship Program for the high school seniors to be allowed to intern on a job they thought they would be interested in as a life-work. I called doctors, hospitals, the police department, lawyers, and other possible places until all the students were placed in a desired place for one semester. Many students went on to choose their internships as their job preference. The businesses that accepted them agreed to evaluate them on their performances at the close of each grading period and at the close of their internships.

After school reading classes for elementary students who were behind their grade level, were started.

A comprehensive testing program for all prospective students was started. We talked about an independent study program for seniors, a four-day school week for them, and several other possibilities. All of these were given up when I left – except the uniforms.

I started teaching beginning Spanish to some elementary students.

When Rev. Clark Card and I started working with some students on our first school annual. The first item that came up was the naming of the book. A long list of names was compiled, but they were all turned down. Finally one day Rev. Card said he thought that it should be named "The Miracle" because it would be a Miracle if a name were chosen. Immediately everybody said, That's it – THE MIRACLE.

The students and Mr. Homer Highsmith chose the name "The Raiders" for the athletics.

When George and I retired after his 65th birthday there were 1,440 students enrolled and we were the largest, private, Christian school in Georgia and the first in Savannah.

_____ Rev. George Akins, _____
Cofounder

Dr. L. Newell Turner
Board Member and Contributor

_____ Miss Anna Clark _____
Principal

Anne Tyson
First Graduate 1952

First Graduation
Top-Left: Joe Latimer, Thomas Harrelson, Buddy Hall, Bill Reagan
Bottom-Left: Gene Porter, Barbara Futch, Millie Farlow, Mary Ann Zealy
Graduate: Anne Tyson

———— Ringing the Rising Bell ————

———— Senior Sneak Day ————

Ardell Jacquot in
"Crown of Thorns" Play

Our Angels on Float in Christmas Parade

Chorus of the Evangelical Bible Institute
Sunday Broadcast 9:00 to 9:30 a.m. on WCCP

High School Chorus and
Director Dottie Sullivan

Early Years
Student Body and Guests

Students in Red Blazers

Horseback Riding

Pool

Girls Partying in Dorm

Elementary Class

First Day in New Dining Room

Dorm

King and Queen of Savannah Christian School

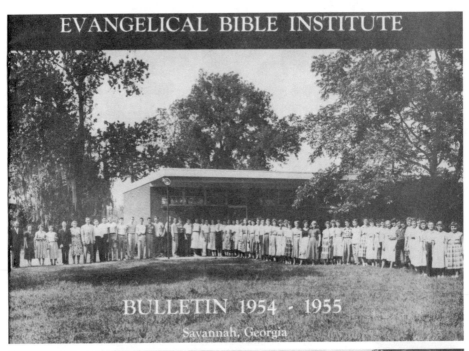

EVANGELICAL BIBLE INSTITUTE

BULLETIN 1954 - 1955

Savannah, Georgia

Savannah Christian High School

Bulletin
1957·1958   Savannah, Georgia

— Bulletin for the School Before and After it Became Savannah Christian —

Savannah Christian Preparatory School

P.O. BOX 2848, CHATHAM PARKWAY   SAVANNAH, GEORGIA 31498   PHONE (912) 233-9607

JOHN F. McGINTY - HEADMASTER

May 30, 1985

The Reverend & Mrs. George Akins
#5 Captain Jim Lane
Savannah, Georgia 31411

Dear Reverend and Mrs. Akins:

The unveiling of the plaque and service honoring you as founders is but a token of our appreciation to you for the many services you have rendered to Savannah Christian Preparatory School.

We are ever endebted to you for giving of yourself for the realization of a dream.

It is my prayer that God will richly bless you in all of your endeavors. I am

Sincerely yours,

John F. McGinty
Headmaster

JFM/jj

enc: (1)

"Savannah's Most Exciting Campus"

Unveiling of the Plaque Honoring the Akins
as Founders of Savannah Christian School

Savannah Christian Preparatory School

Developing the whole person to the glory of God

Daycare-Preschool
Lower School
Middle School
Upper School
E.D.E.N.
Admissions
Alumni
Development
Search
Contact Us

BACK TO SCHOOL

Calendars

Strategic Plan

Uniform Code

SCPS Celebrates 50!

Question: What does it take to put together the biggest birthday party you've ever been to?

Answer: How about 12 buses with full police escort, 8 tents, 22 tables with tablecloths, 200 balloons, 2000 imprinted napkins, 19 sheet cakes, 1800 drinks, 50 pounds of ice, 15 coolers, 2 porta-potties, 6 cans of line marking paint, 55 volunteers, a bullhorn and a mobile crane!

That's how you gather together all of the SCPS school family for the celebration of the half-century! To commemorate our 50th Anniversary, the entire school gathered on the soccer field of the Chatham Parkway campus for an unforgettable image. In the picture above are more than 1800 students (from Daycare through 12th grade), faculty, staff and board members, plus Mrs. Harold Deane Akins and Mr. Elmo Weeks, who have been associated with the school since its founding on September 17, 1951.

It was a beautiful morning, warm with a slight breeze as students from the DeRenne campus arrived and all filed onto the field. Each homeroom found its pre-determined marks on the field, filling each letter and number with amazing precision. What appeared as a mass of "bunched up" humanity from the ground emerged as wonderfully-formed letters and numbers when viewed from the mobile crane high above the crowd.

—————————————— SCPS Celebrates 50 ——————————————

SCPS Athletic/Fine Arts Center Groundbreaking

SCP FIGHT SONG

We are the mighty RAIDERS of SCP.
Better look out for us here we come.
We're gonna fight, fight, fight for a VICTORY tonight,
Just to prove we are NUMBER ONE.

Stand up and cheer for the RED and WHITE.
Show 'em how we out shine all the rest.
We're gonna win this game for the sake of RAIDER fame.
Never fear, we'll always be the BEST.

See the pride of RAIDER country moving down the field,
Thundering, thundering all the way.
We will march to VICTORY just as before.
And when we score, we're gonna shout HOORAY.

We are the MIGHTY RAIDERS of SCP.
Better look out for us, here we come.
We're gonna fight, fight, fight for a VICTORY tonight,
Just to prove that we are NUMBER ONE.

WE'RE NO. 1..

EUROPE IN 1957

Jeremiah 33:3. Call unto me, and I will answer thee, and shew thee great and mighty things, which thou knowest not.

On July 15, 1957, George and I loaded our car and headed for New York, where two days later we were to embark on an adventure that was to last until early September.

My cousin, Adrienne Prankard, who lived near New York, met us at our hotel and brought me the first orchid I ever had. She took our car to her home for the duration.

The next day in New York we met the other members of the Brownell Tour at the hotel and received pertinent information about our tour. Tickets were purchased for special events such as the Opera in Rome, the Follies in Paris, and special activities in the different countries we would visit during the summer. Late in the afternoon, we headed for our ship, the Italia, which was waiting for us in the New York Harbor. I might add right here that the Italia had been advertised as the ship with the greatest food on the Atlantic – and it certainly lived up to its reputation.

Upon arriving at our cabin, we found a beautiful bouquet of flowers sent by the folks back at the school. That was indeed a great send-off.

I shall never forget my emotion as that huge ship began to pull away from the shore, and we were off to the great blue yonder across the ocean. The time of anticipation was over, now the realization. I did not want to change places with anyone in the world. I was really on board the Italia, and on my way to Europe. We were to spend nine days on the Atlantic, but they were not boring days. There was so much activity on board it was hard to keep up. George was invited to be the speaker for the Sunday service, which was a wonderful experience for both of us. Days later we stopped in the harbor at Plymouth, England to take on mail, water, and supplies. Then we were on our way to Le Havre, France.

We disembarked there and boarded the train that would take us to Paris. What an experience that was. The engine burned coal and sent a stream of black smoke behind it right into the windows of our car. When we headed into tunnels, we would all rush to pull down windows to keep from being overcome by smoke. This was in the days before air-conditioned rail cars. We were assigned to cubicles, but many passengers rode in the center aisle of the car sitting on their luggage for the entire trip.

Finally our eyes beheld the great city of Paris. Several days were spent taking in the many historic places. First of all, the newlyweds, Gena and her husband (I have forgotten his name), George and I went to the Eiffel Tower. Gena and I wanted to ride the elevator to the top, but the guys wanted to just sit and watch the crowd. It was finally agreed that they would allow us one hour to go to the top of the tower. We hurriedly got in line at the elevator and there we waited the full hour and never went anywhere. We agreed that we wouldn't tell the men a lie, just not tell the whole story. When they asked what we thought about our adventure, the reply was that Paris looked the same from up there. Riding through the Arc de Triomphe made us feel a wee bit victorious also.

We had all purchased tickets to the Follies before leaving New York. This is the big night that we will actually see the famous Follies. When they played the music to "God Bless the Queen," it reminded us of our song, "My Country 'Tis of Thee" to the same tune. The wives in our tour group were told to "hold on to our husbands" that night to protect them against the scantily clad dancers.

We went to Napoleon's Tomb. He is placed in a position that will cause everyone to "look up to him." We visited the place where the Armistice of World War II was signed and thanked God for that place. We toured the Louvre and saw the Mona Lisa. She looked quite ordinary to me. The gardens around Paris were well kept and quite beautiful.

We would not be traveling by train for the next portion of the journey. Instead we were to transfer to our bus which we would be riding through many different countries.

When I was in Elementary School, my teacher was a German. Her uncle was in charge of a boys' school in Germany, so she suggested that each of us take one of the letters she had received from the boys over there, and write to them. I picked the letter from Kurt Balke because it was so beautifully written I could read his address. We corresponded for many years – in fact, until the war came along, and he had married.

He was soon "missing in action" in World War II and I continued writing to his widow, who along with their daughter Christel met us in Wiesbaden. They traveled all day by train and brought us a beautiful bouquet of yellow roses. They had dinner with us and we had a delightful evening with them at the hotel. They spoke a little English, but we knew only a few words in German. George told Christel that she had a beautiful wrist watch. She replied, "It is no good, it stands still." We told her that it had the right time twice a day.

In Scandinavia, we took a boat train. Our car was loaded onto a ship which carried us to Sweden. Our train then took us through Norway and on down to Denmark. In Norway we had a long visit to Vigeland Park where one man carved in stone the life struggle of men and women from childhood to death. In Sweden we saw the Kon Tiki, the ship that was used by explorer and writer Thor Heyerdahl to travel down the Gulf Stream and 4,300 miles across the Pacific Ocean.

I think Italy and Switzerland were my two favorite countries. The majestic Alps of Switzerland are beyond description. There were so many fantastic places to see in Italy like the Leaning Tower, and the Baptistery next to it.

In the Baptistery, a singer stood in the doorway and demonstrated its special construction. He sang one note acapello which traveled through the building and the sound became that of a full choir.

We also visited the Lido in Venice, the statue of David in Florence, and St. Paul's Basilica in Rome. Since I am not writing a travelogue and I do cover some of these sites in other chapters, I am not going to describe them in depth.

We were in Rome on a Sunday, so George was asked to bring a message to our tour members in the hotel there. There was one disappointment in Italy – we were not able to go into the Sistine Chapel as it was being refurbished.

While touring Europe along the Mediterranean Sea, we went in swimming several times, especially while in France.

Finally we were off to England after going through Austria and Holland. The flower markets in Holland were most spectacular. The fields around the markets were filled with colorful flowers. The Isle of Markham was where the natives still wear wooden shoes and dress like they did years ago. We looked for Hans Brinker, but he must have been off that day. I bought a pair of wooden shoes, but have never worn them.

One day as we were riding along the highway I observed a gate in the middle of a field. with no fence. Behind the gate stood about a dozen cows. I thought that is the dumbest group of cows I have ever seen. Why don't they just walk around the gate? Then I observed that instead of fencing – there were ditches full of water on each side of their paths. Those cows weren't so dumb after all.

But, Oh London. What can one say about that great city. The Palace with the guards, the London Bridge, the Seine and all their famous places – like Piccadilly Circus, and double-deck buses are all wonderful sights to see. It would take many pages to tell all about our experiences there.

While in Europe, we never had ice in any of our drinks. They were refrigerated, but we never had the luxury of ice in our glasses. I remember being thirsty one hot day in Paris, stopping in a shop and ordering a Coke. The clerk, reached up, took one in a white bottle (Cokes should be in green bottles, shouldn't they?) off the shelf, and handed it to me. Oh, how I longed for just one drink with ice in my glass. I think I was being prepared for what was to follow later in Mexico, Guatemala, Egypt, Kenya, and Haiti.

One evening in Rome we had the pleasure of sitting at a table with our tour guide. An Italian lady who teaches school in Egypt during the school year and directs tours for her brother, who owns Oltremare Travel Bureau in Rome. She insisted on treating us to an order of octopus which we had never tasted before.

While in Rome we went to the Opera Aida which is presented in an open-air theater at night. The stage was so large that they had plenty of room for a huge group of performers. We also visited the Isle of Capri, which didn't seem like an island to me. It is a high mountain surrounded by water. That was an experience that I have never forgotten. Frank Sinatra sang so beautifully about that great isle.

We were especially blessed the day that we went to the Blue Grotto on the island of Capri. It was a very calm day otherwise we would not have been able to go into the cave – the entrance is so small it is impossible to enter when the water is rough. A boat load of tourists get into a boat and the man in charge guides the boat through the small opening while we all put our heads down. When inside, we can look toward the cave opening and the light makes the blue water sparkle. It is crystal clear and different from anything I had ever seen.

As we rode a train through Norway, we had a big party in the baggage car. At dinner that evening, we saved parts of our salad to make corsages to wear. There was a lot of creativity among the ladies. It was after we had been to a beautiful marble hall during the afternoon that was often rented for parties and we couldn't party there because our train was leaving in a short while. So we had a party in the baggage car of the train, including making corsages and dressing in our sleeping attire. This was the most unusual and hilarious party – I had ever attended. After seeing all the fabulous sights across the ocean, we came to the conclusion that we Americans are truly the most blessed nation on earth.

Mexico and Guatemala

Proverbs 19:17. *He that hath pity upon the poor lendeth unto the LORD; and that which he hath given will he pay him again.*

In 1968, three students from Savannah Christian School: Vicki Galento, 15, of Tulsa, Oklahoma; Alice Smith, 16, of Hilton Head Island, South Carolina; and Joanne Jarrell, 16, of Charleston, South Carolina; and I loaded my camper and my station wagon and took off on a 7,000 mile trip to Mexico and Guatemala to visit a former student and her parents.

Patty Read, the daughter of missionaries in Chimaltenango, Guatemala had been the roommate of Joanne and had just graduated from *Savannah Christian School.* She and her parents invited us to visit them during the summer.

At the end of our first day on the road, we camped in Valdosta. The girls bought a pooh-pooh cushion, which made a disgusting sound when someone sat on it, and made good use of it the next day. They also bought some black tape and the next morning the following sign greeted me in big letters on the back of the camper: "GUATEMALA OR BUST."

They slept much of the day in the car while I drove, and came alive at night when I needed to sleep. That night we camped in New Orleans and once again they were up late. They were quite surprised the following day when they tried to go to sleep and I awakened them with a pop of a newspaper telling them that a fly was on their head. That did the trick- that night they slept and so we got on a better schedule.

We had much fun in Mexico. The first night there we stopped at a campsite at the foot of a huge mountain. The camp was run by a American man and his Mexican wife. Their daughter took my girls horseback riding and swimming. We really didn't want to leave the next morning, but we had a long trip ahead of us, so off we went.

The first restaurant we ate in (Mrs. Webster's) had the best tacos we had ever eaten.

On to Mexico City where we camped with many Americans. While there, we all got together and went to a Bull Fight. That night was special because the young man, Avera, became a full-fledged bull fighter.

I wanted my two granddaughters to go with us on this trip, but their mother was skeptical of such a wild adventure. My son's comment was, "If anyone can make such a trip, my mother can." In spite of George, Jr.'s encouragement the girls' mother won out and they did not join us.

We went higher into the mountains and farther from the appearances of 20th Century civilization than most travelers. It was truly a scenic and exciting adventure. We often had to stop and let our engine cool a bit because of the high-mountain pulling.

We visited a school for artisans at Santa Maria Del Rio and watched the students (male and female separated on different floors of the building) weave simple blankets and beautiful silk rebozos. They make designs in their weaving, or certain markings on their products identifying where they originated.

Our last night in Mexico was spent parked on the side of a filling station with our electric cord plugged into one of their sockets. Every where we went, we seemed to draw an audience. This stop was no different. We were soon surrounded by children, so we sang some choruses in Spanish and taught them some Bible verses.

As I talked with the children, one little girl told me that four of the children were her brothers and sisters. I remarked that she had a big family. She informed me that there were several more at home.

Mexico is divided into separate sections, and as we passed from one to the other, the men always wanted to look inside our camper. We were a real curiosity to them.

Each day as we parked in Mexico we had to hire a group of children to watch the camper while we went shopping. Their pay was some candy. We were warned in the booklet provided by Sanborn's Travel Service that if we didn't make such an agreement with the children we might have flat tires, or some other damage when we returned.

CHIMALTENANGO, GUATEMALA

After over two weeks on the road, we finally arrived close to our destination. One day we followed a truck carrying Bimbo Bread hoping to catch up with the driver and buy a loaf. We had heard that Bimbo made extra good bread. Alas. That will have to wait for another trip.

We were told earlier that as we got close to the Read's house in Chimaltenango we should send a telegram ahead and give the messenger time to deliver it on his bicycle. It seemed very strange to us. But then, we were in a foreign country without all the amenities of the United States. We sent the telegram and waited for it to be delivered, then continued on to our destination.

We arrived at our destination on the feast day of Saint Ann, patron saint of Chimaltenango. The town was alive with activity. Vendors were selling flowers on every corner; barefoot children ran through the streets; solemn-faced Indians crowded the marketplace.

Patty Read and her parents lived in a nice house. They had the largest and sweetest strawberries in their yard, which was enclosed in a high concrete block fence. The gate was so narrow that I couldn't drive the camper into the yard. The next morning when we walked outside the gate, we discovered someone had taken the chain used to secure the camper to the station wagon. That necessitated a trip to Guatemala City to purchase another one.

As we traveled around Guatemala, and also Mexico, we often had to wait until the chickens, dogs, and other animals were cleared from the road so we could pass through.

We visited the John F. Kennedy School one day. Our U.S. tax dollars paid for the school in Guatemala. We learned the post office opened occasionally. We saw men pushing large yellow cans around. We were told that was the City Sanitation Department. Out of town, the buzzards handled the sanitation.

We picnicked one day at the beautiful Lake Atitlan, a volcano crater lake where we watched a race in dugouts. The top man from each village was competing. That was the coldest water I ever swam in. We had a delicious lunch and fought the awful yellow flies.

We had a delightful day at the El Mercado (market) where we loaded up ponchos, small tables, and wool blankets.

We used every minute of our precious vacation time, absorbing sights and sounds and local color ravenously. With the help of the Reads, who had lived for many years in Guatemala, we were able to sample the culture as natives rather than tourists, eating native food, and visiting the cave of a witch doctor. Three young men were pouring some sort of liquid over a goat, getting ready to sacrifice it.

While I was a student at Georgia Southern, I prepared a paper on race relations and their class distinctions in Guatemala as there is definitely a caste system there.

I observed with special interest the life of the country's Indians. Comprising over half the population of Guatemala, the Indians are bound by strong class distinctions. The difference between an Indian and a Latino is hard for an outsider to understand. To become a Latino, higher in the class system, an Indian merely goes to another village, and puts on shoes and other gentleman's attire - then he can become a Latino, but he cannot become one in his native village.

Guatemala is a beautiful country. It is bordered by mountains on the north and a sea shore to the south. When I saw all the banana trees, I thought, Oh, boy, I'll buy some fresh ones here. But alas, I was told none can be bought here. They ship all of them to the United States.

Our time at the Robinson Bible Institute where the Reads were teachers was very inspiring. We ate there one day and attended a religious service. There I gave my testimony in Spanish for the first time.

At the Institute, we were entertained by Chakchiquel Indians performing an ancient ritual in three languages.

I was amazed at all the good food Mrs. Read could cook on a small two-burner oil stove. She made cakes and biscuits and a delicious tomato stew made with fresh veggies and an egg dropped in the soup for each person eating. I tried several times to duplicate that dish, but I didn't have the same fresh vegetables. She went to the market every morning and bought fresh produce.

Guatemala is famous for its coffee and Orchata, a rice-based drink, which I like very much. There is a restaurant on the Ogeechee Road here in Savannah which now features Orchata.

I first learned about tacos from the Guatemalan students, also the frying of bananas (plantains).

We met Mr. and Mrs. Estrada, the parents of the twins who were enrolled in our school. Mrs. Estrada danced for us in the kitchen where her husband couldn't see her.

While in Guatemala City we went to the American Embassy and had all of our records checked hoping we would not have such a hassle upon our return to the border town of Tapachula. That was only wishful thinking. I had been forewarned by some of the Americans in Mexico City that we would probably have to give a bribe to the *aduano* (border guard) in order to re-enter Mexico.

The *aduano* kept telling me my papers were not in order. He said I would probably have to go back to Guatemala City to the American Embassy. This upset the girls. I told them not to worry, if all else failed, I would shake him up with tears. He walked away for a few minutes, and when he returned he had a written message that read, "For a fee of $10.00 we could proceed." I paid the fee and we were once again on our way home.

On the remote highways, the only traffic was trucks and jeeps. Of course the drivers are men. We were close behind a big truck when we came to a stream where a group of men were swimming without bathing suits. One man was standing beside the road waving to the truck, when suddenly he saw us. I have never seen anyone drop so fast. Obviously, he was startled by the appearance of the four American females.

Traveling through Mexico and Guatemala was made easier than expected by the helpful people we encountered. One man in Monterey drove eight miles out of his way to lead us through town when we asked for directions. And another time, the manager of the restaurant where we were eating got in his car and guided us to the right road.

Kaopectate had been a constant companion for the duration of our trip. Montezuma's Revenge.

Soon we arrived safely back in Georgia with many precious memories.

—————— Laundry Day in Guatemala ——————

El Mercado in Guatemala

Fair Day

Vickie, Me, Alice, Joanne

Guatemala or Bust

———— Mother and Daughter ————

———————— Children at Bible Time ————————

Bull Fight

Rev. Read, Vickie, Joanne, Alice

CAMPING WITH MY GRANDS
AND THEIR GIRL FRIEND

Deuteronomy 23:14. For the Lord thy God walketh in the midst of thy camp... therefore shall thy camp be holy...

When I went to Mexico and Guatemala, I wanted my two granddaughters to go with me, but some members of the family thought it was too dangerous to travel through Mexico, therefore they could not go.

About a year later their dad asked me if I would consider taking them on a camping trip during the summer if he gave me his credit card to pay all the expenses.

I accepted his offer, and began to plan a trip to Canada and all points between. So soon we were off on a wonderful trip. We started in North Carolina where we saw the play, "Unto These Hills" and visited interesting sites. Then on we went to the Mammoth Cave in Kentucky. I had read about this huge cave, but seeing it was by far the greatest experience one could imagine.

Niagara Falls was our destination so when we reached Toronto, we found a good campground and started sightseeing. Of course, the Falls were spectacular. We boarded the boat "The Sea Mist" for a trip under the Falls. We had lunch in the Space Needle that was built for the World's Fair. As we sat there eating our food, we made a complete turn for a panorama view of the whole region. Riding the elevator down on the outside was exciting.

Our next stop was Boston, the site of the famous Boston Tea Party. All of the New England states with their majestic mountains were beautiful. I wish I could have captured some of them on a canvas.

We then made our way on down to New York City, and finally several stops in historic Virginia before returning home. At one point we had to load everything onto a ferry for a trip across the water. The girls thought that was "cool." We came home with many precious memories.

ABOVE AND BEYOND THE CALL OF DUTY

Psalms 56:11. In God have I put my trust: I will not be afraid what man can do unto me.

Not long after the Union Mission bought the Telfair Road property in Savannah, George and I loaded up a two-ton truck with boys and girls for a hay ride to the site.

All went well going out and while we were there. Everyone was having a great time, but when the departure time came, George handed me the keys and told me to drive the truck back to the Mission. I knew nothing about driving such a large truck with different gears, and there stood all those young people looking anxiously at me.

I took the keys reluctantly, climbed up into the driver's seat while George called out my instructions. After I prayed for help from the Lord, we took off. Thank the Lord for answered prayer – we arrived back safely at the Mission.

George had a radio program once a week on WCCP. For some unknown reason, he must have forgotten about the program that week. When the announcer called me and asked me to come take the program, I was completely speechless. Can anyone imagine me speechless? I went in on a prayer and gave a fifteen-minute Bible lesson.

There were a lot of problems when the Mission was in the process of buying the property on the Telfair Road. The man who rented the property went down and took out an option to buy the land as soon as he found out the Mission was planning to buy it. I won't go into all the details, but everyone feared for George's life. When the time came for some legal papers to be served, I was told that it was too dangerous for George to go with John Travis, our lawyer – that I should go.

I drove up to the house, and we saw the man in the yard. He immediately went into the house. John said, "Pray that he isn't going for his gun." He came back out into the yard, and John asked me to hand the papers to him – the man refused to take them. Mr. Travis, said, "Just drop them at his feet. His curiosity will cause him to come get them after we leave." We left there somewhat shaken, but very thankful.

Another time I was asked to take a lunch to a man who was putting up a fence down at the end of a one-lane road into the woods near I-16. I had to back a long way before I had any chance of turning around after handing him his lunch. I am so glad I didn't know about him when I went down that road, but I learned more later that day.

I went to a Sunday school class party that evening and when I returned to the Mission it was completely surrounded by police cars. They were looking for the very man to whom I handed the lunch. He had killed a couple a few miles out of Savannah in Faulkville. The next morning he was captured in a restaurant on Barnard Street. As far as I know, he is still in prison, unless he has died.

On many occasions, my duties were certainly not typical of a principal's duties: I had to cook the meals when the cook was sick and drive the bus when the bus driver was off. When the water pressure on the water tank went down, guess who had to prime the pump – ME.

PART THREE

YEARS OF CHANGE

PURCHASE OF PROPERTY

Ecclesiastes 8:9a. All this have I seen, and applied my heart unto every work that is done under the sun...

One Saturday afternoon in the early 1970s, a man came out to the trailer where we lived on the campus of Savannah Christian School. He told George that he was representing an estate and wondered if George could show him the property line. Of course, he could. George asked him if there was a possibility that the property would be for sale. The man said that any property sale would have to be approved by the family involved. George then asked him if he would give him the first right of refusal if the property was put up for sale.

Not long after that the property along the railroad was for sale. We bought the property because it joined the Savannah Christian land.

We used the proceeds from the sale of that property to purchase our lot on Skidaway Island, later called "The Landings," and to build our house.

We were the second family to move there in December 1973.

AFTER SAVANNAH CHRISTIAN SCHOOL

Proverbs 3:5-6. Trust in the LORD with all thine heart; and lean not unto thine own understanding. In all thy ways acknowledge him, and he shall direct thy paths.

After leaving Savannah Christian School, I was offered various jobs, and finally decided on the Christian school in Ridgeland, South Carolina. My second offer which was to be in charge of a business on Hilton Head for a local firm was most appealing, but after talking with my son, I chose the other path.

I left the Christian school for one reason only - financial. I then went to work for the Jasper County Board of Education. The salary was much higher and the fringe benefits, which I am still enjoying, were wonderful. I worked for them for twelve years until I was 67 years of age.

In the summer before I made the change from a private school to a public school I had started working in the evenings for Draughon's Business College – now South University. I worked for them for seventeen years.

During those years, my friends Gladys Newsome and Ann Lewis decided to sell Tot's Wonderland Day Care Center. I bought the day care center and the two adjoining lots, one of which contained their house. When I went to the bank to get a loan, I was told that I would have to have my husband's signature on the loan. I told them, "No Way." After some further negotiating, I got the loan.

The other day I had to go to a shop on Montgomery Street to pick up a part for my refrigerator. When I arrived at the shop there was a notice on the door, "Will be back in thirty minutes." Instead of waiting there, I decided to visit my old Day Care Center on 61st Street. I am so glad that I did. It is now called "Emmanuel Christian School." Mrs. Sandra King, who bought the property, has enlarged it quite a bit and has a large group of boys and girls who are learning their ABCs in a Christian environment. What a blessing I had there that morning. God bless you always, Mrs. King.

At that time in my life, along came a friend who suggested that I ought to enter the Stock Market. How wonderful her suggestion turned out to be.

While talking with another teacher one evening at South College, we decided to look into the possibility of opening a school supply business. A third teacher soon joined us and as a result we bought some property and opened Classic School Supply. We operated this until Betty moved out of town, Liz's husband died as the result of an accident, and George's health declined so much that I was needed to care for him. We rented the building for a few years and then decided to sell it. It became the office for Tyler Construction Company, and now Colony Bank.

How I thank the Lord for leading me along the right path to secure my future as I had nothing when I left Savannah Christian. In fact, I was in debt for a car because I had to leave the old Government Surplus Vehicle that I had been using at the school.

OUR MOVE TO THE LANDINGS ON SKIDAWAY ISLAND

Matthew 18:20. For where two or three are gathered together in my name, there am I in the midst of them.

The first time George and I saw Skidaway Island was when President and Mrs. Nixon, along with Julie and David Eisenhower came to the Island. We had a special invitation to attend from one of our Board members. The Nixons came to the Island by boat and left by helicopter which was parked very close to our seats. This was before the road was paved and it was quite dusty that day; however, the program was wonderful.

On another occasion, George, George, Jr., Barbara, and I came by boat. We came ashore and got a good look at the beauty of this virgin Island.

When we retired from Savannah Christian School, we bought a lot on the Island which had been named "The Landings" and started building our small retirement home.

The Little family was the first family to move to the Island and Roger and Sue Hard and the Akins joined the Littles on December 8, 1973.

It was a beautiful, virgin island, but quite desolate at that time. There were no guards, no paved streets, and an abundance of wild animals. There was a lot of good hunting on Skidaway Island as we often had wild turkeys, deer, hogs, opossum, and raccoon in our yard. Our builder used generators to build our house, but electricity came the week we moved in.

Shortly after we moved in, I was shopping at McCrory's department store and saw sets of beautiful blue water glasses that would perfectly match the blue and white striped wallpaper in my new kitchen. The glasses were for sale for $2.98 for a set of four. I needed eight but could only afford one set of four. I have kept one glass as a reminder of God's blessings upon us since that time.

The island workers were busy pouring the curbstone in preparation for the paving of the roads.

Houses began popping up like weeds in a spring garden. George and I saw the need for some form of church services on the Island, as there were no churches for several miles.

We were offered the use of The Landings' Marshwood Club, which was now finished, and furnished coffee and sweet rolls for the Sunday Services. George either preached on Sunday morning or invited a guest speaker for the services. At Easter we had a Sunrise Service near one of the lagoons. As the congregation grew, we organized and bought a piano, which I played for the services. The piano was given to the Skidaway Island Presbyterian Church after they built their church and we gave up the work.

There are now several thousand people living on the island, and there are only a little over 300 lots left for sale.

I have seen many changes to The Landings since we moved out here. Instead of one club – the Marshwood – there are three more clubs, The Plantation, Deer Creek, and Oakridge. I understand these additions make The Landings the largest private club in America.

There are 36 tennis courts, six championship golf courses, two marinas, a Library, a Fitness Center, a Village of commercial buildings, several churches, two outdoor Olympic-size swimming pools, a dog park, and a ball field. I hope I have not left anything out.

The Littles, the Hards, and George have all passed away, so now I have been living here at The Landings longer than any other person – thirty-three years in December 2006.

GEORGE AND I AND. . .GOLF

1 Samuel 16:17. And Saul said unto his servants, Provide me now a man that can play well, and bring him to me.

Many years ago, George and I visited our family when they lived in Atlanta. They always planned special ways to entertain us. One night George, Jr. suggested that he and his Dad try a game of night golf. Both of them were very athletic and they played many different sports, but George, Sr. had never tried golf. That game opened up a new avenue of activities for my husband.

When we returned home, George always found time to practice hitting balls around the campus of Savannah Christian School.

After George retired and we moved to The Landings, I continued to work two jobs – one a day job and the other a night job. This gave George an opportunity to practice his golf every day. There were only a few people living at The Landings in those early years. Some days George played up to fifty-four holes of golf. He became quite good at the game, and as the population increased, he had more competition. On Saturdays he often won the cash prize for leading the pack.

George kept trying to get me interested in the game, but after working and doing all my chores, I had very little enthusiasm to take on golf. I finally gave in, and he started teaching me. I bought golf shoes, a golf bag, and all the necessary equipment.

George was quite serious about his game. He played to win, but I, on the other hand, played for the fun of it.

We used to go out early in the mornings before the course was crowded. One beautiful Saturday morning we were out there. When it was my time to tee off, I hit the ball straight to the left bunker. George proceeded to lecture me. "Why did you hit the ball into the bunker?" he asked. I just laughed. That caused more questions. "Did you line up your ball?" "Did you keep your head down?" On and on, he went. I still laughed. "With that wide, beautiful fairway, how could you go straight to the left?" I continued to laugh. I really thought it was funny that he gave such a long lecture about one little ball taking its own path to the left bunker. I had seen other players do the same thing, *including George.*

This is the clincher. When he got up to tee off, I stood there anxiously waiting to see where his ball would go. To my glee, his ball went straight to the right bunker I joyfully exclaimed, "Oh, I finally see what I did wrong – I went to the *wrong bunker.*" He looked at me over his glasses, and we both just stood there laughing.

One Sunday after church a friend asked me to play a round of golf with her. At first I declined, but I finally gave in. On one of the holes it was my time to putt. I really didn't expect to make it – it was such a long putt, and to my dismay, our golf pro just stopped his golf cart and watched. I couldn't believe it when my ball went straight into the hole. That was the greatest putt I ever made and the pro saw it. He spread the news around that I was such a super putter. I didn't tell him that was the only one like that I ever made.

A few months later the club offered a clinic to all the ladies. I was still working and had to give a reason for my absence – even though we were allowed days off each year. I finally went to the office and told the secretary that I was going to the clinic the next day. She assumed it was the health clinic, and I never explained.

The next day, the pro was having each lady hit a ball out of the bunker. Of course, I was the leader. I had been in the bunkers so many times I had more practice and won.

EGYPT AND ISRAEL

Luke 2:4-5. And Joseph also went up from Galilee, out of the city of Nazareth, into Judaea, unto the city of David, which is called Bethlehem; To be taxed with Mary his espoused wife, being great with child. And so it was, that, while they were there, the days were accomplished that she should be delivered. And she brought forth her firstborn son, and wrapped him in swaddling clothes, and laid him in a manger; because there was no room for them in the inn.

Margaret Whiting's old hit tune that says, "Far away places with strange sounding names, far away over the sea" has called to me from childhood. When we lived on the campus of Savannah Christian all those years, every time a train blew its whistle on the track near our house, I wished I were on a trip going to those far away places that continually called me.

In 1980. George, Jr. and his wife arranged for George and me to join them on a trip of our dreams – Egypt and Israel.

The plan was that we were to meet them at Kennedy Airport in New York. We were scheduled to arrive first and were to go to the concourse where they would be coming in from Miami for an evening flight to Rome. We got to New York early in the day at the appointed place, but they didn't. They had all the tickets and plans for the trip. Also, this flight was the only one until the next Thursday. It is needless to say – we were getting a little anxious as the sun went down.

During all this time that elapsed, I was constantly in touch with the airline rep trying to find out what was happening – or not happening.

I told George that we should go on to the point of departure and wait there. That involved taking a bus to another concourse, but proved to be a wise decision. Shortly after we got there, an anxious George Jr. arrived followed by Barbara. Their flight from Miami had been cancelled, and they had to have two passengers headed to New York bumped from their flight in order for them to arrive in time for our overseas flight. They had never looked as good to us as they did at that moment.

We soon took off, and arrived in Roma the next morning where we had a layover of several hours. During those hours we had to listen to a small child scream continuously. The airport officials tried many ways to quiet the child, but were unsuccessful. My husband said that if that baby got on our plane, he was not getting on it. The child was left behind, and we flew away – next stop Cairo, the city that truly comes alive at night.

There are nearly twenty million people living in Cairo. The traffic jams are very annoying and those Cairenes have hot tempers. Everyone in that city lives for the wonderful evenings.

We went to our hotel, checked in and got ready for our evening meal. George. Jr. was always the meal arranger wherever we were. He planned an evening meal on the veranda overlooking the Nile. The setting was very relaxing, but as for the meal, the waiter spoke no English and just smiled as we asked questions. We had no idea what we were eating, but we were hungry.

It was September and everything was covered with dust as there had been no rain so far that year in Cairo.

Egypt is famous for its antiquity. King Tut's display at the museum was back in Cairo after its American Tour. The Valley of the Kings and the Valley of the Queens were somewhat alike. The walls of both were covered with hieroglyphics, which include the figures of plants and animals painted or drawn in beautiful colors. Both Valleys were cut out of mountains.

The Pyramids and the Great Sphinx of Giza are among the most famous places in Egypt. The Sphinx is a huge monument with the head of a human and a lion's body. I didn't realize there were three pyramids until I saw them. How the Egyptians were able to move the heavy stones with manpower only to build the Pyramids is still unknown. Our guide told us that even the placement of the pyramids is still a mystery.

We all rode very dirty camels up to the Pyramids. Riding a camel is not the fun I thought it would be. It was hard for me to get on and off that rascal. We had to use flashlights to go down the steps into the large room. We went to a Sight and Sound Show at the Sphinx in the evening. We sat in the bleachers where a Savannah lady had been robbed and seriously injured not too long before we were there. My evening was spent almost entirely on a self-imposed lookout. I didn't want any of us to be victims.

We flew to Abu Simbel, a city in southern Egypt, and there boarded the Sheraton Nile Cruise Ship, the Aton for the cruise up the Nile River discovering the wonders of Ancient Egypt. The ride up the river, going through the locks of the canal that Russia had built in Egypt was my first trip through locks. We all stood on the deck to watch the water either lift our ship, or lower it as the locks were opened, or closed.

Visiting Memphis with the huge obelisks lying flat on the ground is still a mystery. How the Egyptians moved stones and built huge objects, with no modern machines is hard to believe, even after seeing the results of their cunning workmanship. As we traveled up the Nile we stopped at Karnak and Luxor. In every picture that was taken of me, I have my bottle of water in my arms. That was truly a necessity, not a luxury in the dry, humid, hot air.

We had to take off our shoes, or cover them, before entering some places of worship. Our heads also had to be covered.

I have had the privilege of traveling to many countries with my family. The one that George, Jr. and I were particularly fascinated with was Egypt.

Then we flew over the Red Sea to Israel. On our El Al flight, we were served a lunch in a small plastic container. I shall always remember the dry, white bread sandwich that was the main part of the meal.

After seeing the Sahara and all the dry land of Egypt, what a contrast Israel was. There were orange groves, fertile fields, lots of trees – and very clean cities.

After settling in for the night, the next morning a bus picked us up for our trip into the City of Jerusalem. As we neared the city, our Tour Guide stopped the bus and said that we should get off the bus and walk into that great city. That was the proper way to enter Jerusalem. Though we were all strangers, we bonded as we walked into that great city together.

There is no adequate way to prepare for that first sight of Jerusalem. Shared by Christian, Jew, and Moslem it is the world's most beloved city. Christian pilgrims traditionally enter the walled Old City by St. Stephen's Gate. There they begin to tread the Via Dolorosa, the path Christ followed on the way to Calvary, or Golgotha where he was crucified. There are fourteen Stations of the Cross along this route. Jerusalem's wealth of religious treasures is so staggering that it would take many years to see all of them. The Western Wall, also known as the Wailing Wall, is believed to be one of the walls of the Temple Mount built by King Herod. As I sat in an area near the wall, I saw many people going up to the wall and placing their prayers in the cracks in the wall.

In the new city we visited the Knesset, Israel's seat of government which holds paintings and sculpture by the nation's greatest artists.

Air-conditioning has spoiled we Americans so much it is hard to realize there are public buildings in the world without it, but we entered several of them. This was years ago, and I imagine they have all been air-conditioned in the interim.

Just outside Jerusalem there is a memorial to John F. Kennedy. Fifty-one pillars sweep upward in the shape of a truncated tree, representing a life cut short.

Before we left on this trip, a fellow-teacher at South College told me to be sure to go to Masada. It was a side-trip, but well worth the time. When we got to the top of the mountain, the guide gave George, Jr. some information about Masada and asked him to read it for all of us. It told about the sufferings of the Jewish people who were living on the top of the mountain for safety. It was an ancient mountaintop fortress in south east Israel on the south west shore of the Dead Sea.

We took a night cruise on the Sea of Galilee. We could have enjoyed it more if the loud music on the boat had been lowered several notches. The Dead Sea was where we had a chance to go swimming. The smell of the water was not very pleasant in the shower room, but we didn't notice the odor so much when outdoors. We visited the Dome of the Rock where its huge cupola gleams like a giant's golden thumb. It is hard to say what the greatest part of this trip was – everything was awesome.

George and I had longed to see Jerusalem and Bethlehem for many years. To see the place where our dear Lord was born, the place of the Crucifixion, the Dead Sea Scrolls (where we were all frisked before entering), the Memorial to the Children, the Holy Mount, and the Upper Room. As the four of us stood in that room where Jesus sat with his disciples, I thought of Thomas coming in and his conversation with Jesus. Imagine touring this historic country with your family. What could be better than that? I think every minister should visit the Holy Land. It truly makes the Life of Christ so very real and personal.

While in Israel, George Jr. received word that the son-in-law of his best friend was killed in a diving accident in North Carolina. We planted a tree in his honor while in Israel.

This trip will always have a special place in my heart and my life. The life of Christ is more real now than ever before.

Pyramid in Egypt

Cairo

Memphis Ramses

Valley of the Queens

Valley of the Kings

Via Dolorosa

Dome

Wailing Wall

Upper Room

Tiberias, Sea of Galilee

River Jordan

Along Lebanese Border

Bunkers Golan

Fiftieth Wedding Anniversary

Psalms 118:24. This is the day which the Lord hath made; we will rejoice and be glad in it.

When the date of our Fiftieth Wedding Anniversary was approaching, our son asked George and me how we wanted to celebrate it. "Would you like a big party?" Before I could say a word, George, Sr. said that he wanted to go to Scotland to see where his ancestors came from.

Therefore, George, Jr. and Barbara planned a tour of Scotland and England.

Our trip started in London. We went to a play entitled "Run for Your Wife." It was a hilarious play which we all thoroughly enjoyed.

We unexpectedly arrived in London when the Queen's Birthday was being celebrated. We saw the great parade where thousands waited in hopes of seeing the Queen. We had the privilege of seeing the Changing of the Guard at Buckingham Palace, many huge magnificent government buildings, and finally Westminster Abbey which we had seen in 1957.

One thing I remembered from my first visit was the fact that some great people are buried there. David Livingstone, who opened Africa to the Gospel is one of the greatest. As we walked down one aisle, we walked over a grave. I didn't feel comfortable doing that. I have always been careful not to walk on a grave, if at all possible. That may be just one of my phobias.

The building is quite spectacular. As we stood there, I imagined what it was like to attend a coronation, or a wedding there. Guests from all over the world would be there dressed in the finest clothing and jewelry. What a privilege the elite have.

We also went to St. Martin's in the Fields Church, the church in London which our church, the Independent Presbyterian Church used as a pattern for its building.

We shopped in the famous Harrod's Department store which is

so large it overwhelmed me. I didn't expect to see a meat market in a famous department store, but there it was. The basement is where one can buy unusual and exotic cuts of meat.

There is no way that we would leave London without having lunch at a Pub. All tourists have that on their "To Do List" right along with getting a hamburger at Piccadilly Circus.

After a few days there, we boarded a train in Victoria Station and started through England where we toured many castles and then headed for Scotland. We saw beautiful purple and yellow fields of Heather and Broom as we were making our way to the Highlands of Scotland.

We searched diligently for the Loch Ness Monster, but he, or she, was no where to be found. So we asked our guide, "When does the Loch Ness monster appear?" "Usually after the fifth shot of whiskey," replied the guide. Now I understand why we never saw the Loch Ness monster during our trip to Scotland.

We went all the way up to the Isle of Skye where we were thankful for the warm boat ride and heavy coats. I bought a wool coat in Aberdeen.

Our son arranged for us to have a big party in Edinburgh for our anniversary. He asked our Tour Guide to call ahead to the hotel and arrange for the four of us to have a special, private dinner and a big party after dinner so everyone on the tour could help us celebrate.

After all of us had eaten, we gathered around the table where our Anniversary cake, and drinks were laid out. We had a great time singing many of the old Scotch songs.

I must add that it was the most unusual anniversary we had in the sixty-one years we were together. I will admit that I would rather have been at home with family and friends on the occasion; however, we did have a great Fiftieth Celebration.

The next morning we toured Edinburgh. We went to the park to see the famous floral clock, the oldest in the world. That clock really had hands that pointed out the time over the 35,000 colorful flowering plants.

There is also a large statue to John Knox in that park, however, he is not buried there. Knox is the person who led the Protestant Reformation in Scotland. Under his leadership, the Church of Scotland adopted a declaration of faith, a form of government, and a liturgy.

Barbara With Lochness Monster

Floral Clock in Edinburgh

Barbara and George, Jr. With Bagpiper

George and I Arrive Back in Miami and Meet Our
Only Great-Granddaughter For the First Time

NEW ZEALAND AND AUSTRALIA

Numbers 14:21. But as truly as I live, all the earth shall be filled with the glory of the Lord.

When so many of our friends were taking trips "down under," I decided that we should go, too. George, Jr. and Barbara were unable to go with us on this trip because of business engagements; however, they provided the first class air fare for us. What a trip.

It is the only time we ever took an overseas tour without a guide. We truly had to rely on our own resources and common sense especially when going through customs at the different points of entrance. This was also the last trip that George and I took together outside of the United States.

I had enjoyed my trip to Hawaii with Doris Hurd, a fellow teacher at South College so much, that I was delighted to be able to take George there and enjoy it with him. Doris and I went to all three islands, but George saw only Honolulu where Pearl Harbor is located..

We flew from Honolulu to Auckland, New Zealand, the city known as the "City of Sails." The harbor was full of boats, which formed a beautiful picture as we flew over on our way to the airport.

On this part of our tour we crossed the International Dateline and lost a day. Don't worry, we get it back on the return trip.

Before we left Savannah, we were given the option of purchasing tickets to a restaurant in New Zealand, which is famous for its lobster. We bought our tickets, and were very glad we did. We arrived in the city after dark, on a very cold night. We had to walk several blocks, but it was warm inside as there was a pot-belly stove in the center of the room that made it very cozy. I have never tasted lobster that delicious anywhere else in the world. I have no idea how it was cooked, but that is one recipe that I wish I had.

We spent several days in Auckland before boarding the bus that took us over the North Island. We traveled through rolling countryside to Waitomo where we saw the spectacular Glowworm

Grotto. Unfortunately the ceiling was very low and rough. George hurt his head so we had to make a side-trip to a doctor to have him checked. We continued on to Rotorua, where we visited Rainbow Trout Springs and then went to Whakarewarewa where the boiling mud pools, geysers, and thermal activity fascinated us. That evening in our hotel we enjoyed the traditional Maori Hangi, whereby the food is cooked underground via steam. Miss New Zealand sang several songs for us that night. She was followed by a concert of dances, songs, and war chants of their culture.

It might be interesting for me to tell you more about the geysers. They are huge holes in the ground through which hot steam pours out from the boiling water within. Food is placed in wire baskets and lowered into the hole where it is cooked. Most of the buildings around the geysers are covered with beautiful Maori woodwork with carvings.

Before leaving, we went to a sheep shearing at Rainbow Farm. The sheep also put on a spectacular program on the stage. They marched up in single file and went to their own spot. At a signal they would turn around, sit down, or do some other command. It was amazing to watch a man shear a large animal in just a few minutes. Of course, New Zealand is famous for its beautiful rugs.

The next morning we again boarded the bus and headed on down to the port where we left the bus and took the ship to Wellington. We had been warned that the trip over that body of water could be extremely rough. I don't care much for riding over very rough seas, since I had already ridden out the tail end of a hurricane coming back from Europe in 1957. I was very happy when we crossed over on an unusually calm day.

As our bus pulled in to Wellington and we saw the round government building in front of us, we were told that it is round so no politician can end up in a corner.

The South Island of New Zealand is one of the most beautiful places I have ever visited. What can compare with Milford Sound? No wonder a whole day was set aside to spend on a boat traveling around the sound. Lunch was also served on the boat. We were there on a clear day so we could see the different animals lying out on the rocks in the sun. The Sound is surrounded by massive peaks rising from the still, clear water. There are secret valleys and waterfalls that add to its beauty.

Mount Cook National Park was our next stop. It was named for Captain Cook the famous explorer who visited many islands along the Pacific Ocean. Even on a cloudy day, Mount Cook defies description.

We passed serene lakes and grassy valleys, stopping in magnificent Queenstown, New Zealand's major holiday resort. The Remarkable Mountains are all lined up and still covered in snow, even though it is summertime.

In New Zealand deer are raised as we raise cows here in America. Every day we could get deer meat sandwiches or have a piece of cooked deer meat for lunch or dinner. We also had pumpkin soup with every lunch and dinner while there. One of the most delightful experiences we had was stopping for hokey pokey ice cream, which is made by adding crunchy pieces of toffee to vanilla ice cream.

Our last day in New Zealand we arrived in Christchurch, the South Island's largest city. and also the most English city in New Zealand.

We then boarded the plane that took us to Sydney, Australia's oldest, largest, and liveliest city. Upon arrival, we completed Customs and Immigration formalities before continuing to our hotel.

The next morning we went across the famous Sydney Harbor Bridge to Manly to see and feed koala bear, kangaroos, emus, wombats and dingoes. George and I held koalas for pictures, and they lived up to their reputation – they slept right through our picture taking. While in Australia we learned that the Australian Air Lines have pictures of kangaroo on all of their planes. Kangaroos can only go forward, never backward.

We also visited the famous Opera House, which has no elevator. Why would they build such a great multi-floored building with only steps to go up or down?

Late one afternoon we were treated to a special show on Phillip Island as the Fairy Penguins put on their nightly parade as they came ashore after a day out in the ocean. We sat in the bleachers and watched them scamper ashore to their holes in the sand where they would spend the night.

We spent some time just walking on the beautiful beaches and enjoying the sunshine. In some parts of Australia it was still snowing and there was much snow still on the mountains of New Zealand.

We took the optional cruise on Sydney Harbor where we were served a wonderful lunch. It is true they do not take American Express Credit Cards on that tour.

On our return trip to Honolulu, we were side-tracked to Fiji, because of a medical emergency on board. This gave us an extra glimpse of that tropical island.

Glow Worm Cave

Sheep On Stage

Sailboats in Auckland Harbor

Round Government Building

Steam Coming Up in Rotorua

Geyser in Rotorua

Opera House in Sidney, Australia

Bridge in Sidney

Kangaroo

George, Sr. at the Ski Slope

LATER YEARS

Psalms 16:11. Thou will show me the path of life: in Thy presence is fullness of joy: at Thy right hand are pleasures evermore.

Jeremiah 33:3. Call unto me and I will answer thee, and show thee great and mighty things, which thou knowest not.

The summer after George passed away (1999), I bought a computer. It was a new toy, but not too easy to really use and enjoy for quite a while. My friend, Al Naismith and I, took two computer classes that were offered to senior citizens through Candler Hospital.

During that summer, I learned that there were many of our church members who were either living in nursing homes or confined to their homes.

I decided that was something I could do – visit them. I bought fruit, bagged it, and took the bags to the shut-ins. One lady, a member of our church living in Azalealand Nursing Home, told me that was the only fresh fruit she had in a long time. She ate it like she thought someone might take it from her.

I always carried my Bible and asked if I could read a few verses for them and have prayer with them. They all agreed.

After a short visit, I was the one who went away happy. I believe they blessed me more than I blessed them.

One Sunday I visited Camilla Clifton, one of our former church secretaries, in a nursing home near Charleston, South Carolina. I had a delightful visit with her, read some scripture, and offered a prayer. She then asked, "May I pray for you?" What a blessing she was.

Most of them have passed away. I hope my visits made their lives a little more joyful.

George used to give out gospel tracts nearly everywhere he went. I followed his example and did this until the Powers That Be, declared this not acceptable in America.

EUROPE 2000

Not long after George passed away, George. Jr. called and told me that he and Barbara were planning to go to Germany to pick up a new car. After that, they were planning to drive around Europe and would like for me to go with them. It didn't take me several days to sign on. I immediately asked, "When do we leave?" Little did either of us realize then how much more would be added to that trip.

We learned that Expo 2000 would be going on during that time in Hanover, Germany. Then we also learned that the famous Passion Play, which is given every ten years, would be going on in Oberamagau, Germany.

Last, but not least, my brother and his wife would be in Rome at the same time we would.

One day George called me and asked if I had one of those new style suitcases with the pull-up handle. I told him that I did not. He told me to go get one. So, I went and bought one. When I put it in the trunk of my car it filled over half of the trunk. I immediately wondered how three of us could travel over Europe with one suitcase in the trunk. Where would the other two go? However, I was assured that it was okay. So I just smiled to myself and thought – my fun is coming when we get to Hanover- when we start loading the car. Sure enough, we all took our luggage out and since George was not only the driver, he was also the Red Cap to load everything.

I got in and waited for the fun I had been anticipating for several months. As I sat and listened to him huffing and puffing and trying to rearrange suitcases, I was waiting for my big moment. It came sooner than I expected.

George, Jr. put his head in the back window and said, "Mom, I have a problem."

I asked, "What problem?"

He replied, "I can get only one suitcase in the trunk. Do you think you can ride there with two suitcases?" I replied that if they were turned sideways, I thought I could.

Later that day I said, "George, if I had known you invited me to travel all over Europe in the baggage compartment, I might not have come." We all had a good laugh.

It wasn't really so bad. Barbara and I changed places often.

The Expo was greater than I had imagined. There were so many pavilions from the different countries. The most outstanding was the one from Japan. Theirs was constructed of recycled white paper. After the Expo closed it was to again be recycled. Mexico had a huge one. Even Cuba had one. They had a small one where a Cuban man sat and rolled cigars which he would then sell to the visitors. The United States did not have a pavilion. We were told that funds were not available.

After leaving the Expo, we traveled down the Fairy Tale Highway through the magnificent mountains of Germany all covered in the luscious green of spring. Each day we got out our map and decided where we wanted to go. What a way to travel — no long lines or delays of trains, planes or buses.

I had looked forward to seeing the famous Passion Play since I was a teenager, and it was more than I had even imagined. It lasted six hours and was entirely in German. The cost for that day was $900 for the three of us, including meals and lodging. We had booklets printed in English so that we could follow the acts. We had front-row seats and when the crucifixion scene took place – right on schedule – a bolt of lightening struck. It was so real – it was hard to believe it was just a part of the play.

On the fourth of July in Germany what does an American do to celebrate? George, Jr. suggested that we have lunch in the nearby *biergarten* (beer garden). They are to Germany, what pubs are to England. We went in and picked out a well-aged, but clean table, in the middle of the room. We were soon served a tasty meal of meat and veggies. Two of us had ordered beef, and the other pork. While we were eating, we enjoyed the music being played by an ensemble. We were delighted when they played our national anthem. That truly gave us a "touch of home" on July 4.

After traveling through the regal mountains of Germany, we made our way down to Italy which was to be our main vacation area.

We spent one day at beautiful Lake Garda. It was the most relaxing day of our trip. We shopped and we ate.(Barbara and I really enjoyed the *gelati* (ice cream). George, Jr. said that if he ever lost us, he was sure to find us at the ice cream shop. We watched the swans swimming, and the boats coming and going. Gentle breezes caressed our tired bodies; soon we were ready to go on toward the south.

Then we traveled on down to Forli, Italy, where we were the guests of Gabriele Ghetti at Gamma Arredamenti, a leading Italian furniture manufacturer. There we were treated like royalty. We had a chauffeur, were treated to several spectacular meals – one dinner in the beautiful Resort of Cervia in an open-air restaurant on the shore of the Adriatic Sea which was unbelievable. I shall never forget that night. We had a seven-course meal. While we were eating, I noticed a waiter over at a middle table. He had a metal pan and was beating up whatever was in it. After a few minutes the food substance, whatever it was, was tossed from the pan and then returned to the pan just like a master pizza maker tosses his dough. I called George's attention to it, and he, too was fascinated at what he saw. The waiter repeated this several times, and each time it was tossed quite a distance from the pan, but it always landed back in the pan without help.

We were given a grand tour of the Gamma Arredamenti leather factory that makes such beautiful leather furniture. I sat on a white leather sofa that sells for $10,000. I'll never own one, but I sat on one. What an experience.

Our next stop was Florence where the famous statue of David still stands. We had the best *lasagne* there that we ever had. The meat was seasoned to perfection, and the dough was soft and covered with tomatoes and a good Italian cheese. Those Italians know how to bake a perfect *lasagne*.

The famous Leaning Tower of Pisa was still leaning; however, they have been trying to drill large boulders under it to keep it from completely falling over. It is a magnificent structure and the Baptistery next to it is another beautiful site I saw for the first time in 1957, forty-three years earlier.

A long time ago, I heard a comedian say that his wife thought Europe was one big shopping center. George, Jr. thought Barbara and I felt that way, but when we got to the leather shops in Florence, George was the big spender and encouraged me to buy a leather jacket that I would never have bought on my own. I'll admit I have enjoyed wearing it for six years now.

Then we were off to one of my favorite cities in the world – Roma, where we were soon settled into our hotel and called my brother and his wife. We took a taxi and met them at their hotel and had dinner with them there. All of us talked about our families and our trip thus far. We each told what we had enjoyed the most, and what was next on our schedule.

Rome was as exciting as ever. Someone once said, "All roads lead to Rome." It is called the "Eternal City" and is built on seven sprawling, green hills, and has so many wonderful places to visit, with the Vatican and all the other famous places.

One evening, while reading my Bible in the hotel room which had a TV, a computer, and a printer in my bedroom. Also a TV, bath robes, and slippers in the bathroom – I was reading about one of my favorite Bible Characters – Paul. When that great man of God was in Rome – he was in stocks in prison.

That is where he wrote the Book of Ephesians, the first of the Prison Epistles and here I was living the life of Riley. What have I ever done to deserve God's blessings? I couldn't help but weep tears of thanksgiving to my Heavenly Father for His blessings to me. The next day we went to Saint Paul's Basilica where Paul is buried. We went back for another look at the Coliseum.

The Catacombs, with the fish on the wall, is another place that touched my heart. There are so many outstanding places to visit while in Roma. I have already been there three times, and I still marvel at its greatness. Excavations are still going on so there may still be more to see in the future.

On this trip we were able to go into the Sistine Chapel which was being restored when we were there in 1957. As we walked from room to room we saw the best of Michelangelo's work. We were told that he painted the ceiling while lying on his back on the scaffold. We spent a long time there marveling at the magnificence of all of it. His talent was unequalled in all the world.

My son has long had a reputation for being able to find the best restaurants in any city. One day on this trip he walked Barbara and me so far to find the perfect place he had to call a cab to take us back to our car.

The next morning we prepared to leave. George, Jr. planned for us to go have another special Italian lunch; however, I had other plans. After two weeks of eating elegant Italian foods, I wanted a change. We were staying on the top of one of the seven hills, and at the bottom of that hill there was a McDonald's. I wanted to go there for a hamburger. Even though George, Jr. thought I was crazy, he walked down the hill with me (for my protection), and waited while I had one of the best hamburgers I ever had -along with a coke and ice cream, which cost me about $1.50 in American money. I was then ready to head for the airport.

I came home broke, but happy.

I felt closer to the Lord and to Peter and Paul in Rome than anywhere else. What they suffered and how little we have suffered for the furtherance of the Gospel. My prayer is still that I may have the privilege of leading more souls to the Lord. That brings more joy than diamonds, silver, or gold.

I said, *"Arrivederci a Roma,"* hoping to return some day.

Leaning Tower and
Corner of the Baptistery

Inside Japan's Pavillion

Mountains In Germany

4th of July in Germany

Waiting for Passion Play to Begin

George, Jr., Gabrielle and Family

Barbara and I at Beautiful Italian Beach

David

My Precious Pets

Ecclesiastes 9-4. For to him that is joined to all the living there is hope: for a living dog is better than a dead lion.

I have a Boykin Spaniel who has beautiful chocolate-colored wavy hair and brown eyes which are encircled with a golden ring. She is now five years old and her name is Tori. She came to me through a friend whose sister-in-law, Jane Naismith, lives on the Isle of Hope in Savannah.

Jane invited us to go see the puppies, two males, and one female. I went to see her with my friend and picked her out when she was just two weeks old. She came to live with me about four weeks later. She has added much joy to my life. When she comes and puts her head on my knee and looks up at me with those adoring eyes – she gets forgiven instantly for whatever she has done.

I also have a black and white tuxedo cat that came to me from Boca Raton, Florida. My son, who loves animals as much as I do, was on his way home from work and rescued him after an accident involving a car driving in front of him. He was just a little kitten and evidently his nose touched the tire of the car and he was thrown up into the air. When he fell onto the road his breath was knocked out of him.

George thought he had been seriously hurt so he quickly stopped the traffic, grabbed a towel from the trunk of his car, picked him up, and rushed him to a nearby vet. He told the vet to do whatever he could to save him. The next morning when George called him, he was told there was nothing wrong with the kitten – except he had a skinned nose.

George called me and asked me if he had someone bring him as far as Daytona Beach, would I meet them there and give "Lucky" a home. I did, and now he has been living with me almost two years. I love him very much. I keep telling him since I had to give him a home, I am very happy that he is such a pretty cat.

The only problem is – Tori doesn't want him living here – hence I have to keep them separated. So far we have managed to all live under the same roof, not always happily. I feared for Lucky's life twice when he went into the kitchen while Tori was there. She grabbed him behind his neck and I had to jump in and pull her away. She wanted to grab me, but I got away in time.

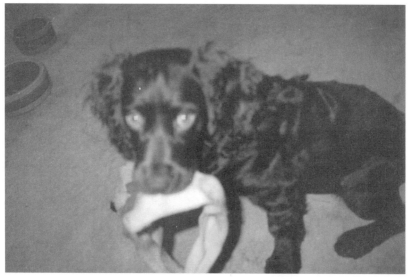

Tori With Toy

Lucky, My Cat

ALUMNI MEETINGS OF STUDENTS FROM THE 1950s

Psalms 150:6. Let every thing that hath breath praise the Lord. Praise ye the Lord.

The first alumni meeting of the Savannah Christian School that I recall was held on August 14, 1981 at Williams Seafood Restaurant. It was so good to see so many of the students who had graduated in the 1950s. The meal was delicious and the fellowship the greatest.

The second one was held in a restaurant on Abercorn with Mr. and Mrs. Ardell Jacquot, two of our earliest teachers. Ardell gave an inspiring message and Dottie entertained us with several piano selections. She was one of the best when she was with us, and she still is. I understand she is now doing a lot of recordings for the Bible Broadcasting Network (BBN). Many of the former students attended with their partners. Rev. William Reagan was one of the planners for this inspiring reunion. George, Sr. and I were there along with Miss Rose Payne.

The third alumni meeting was planned by Alida Lois, who is now operating a business in Atlanta. The meeting was held at the Johnny Harris Restaurant and, if I remember correctly, there were about thirty-five persons present.

There was a sadness that evening because Albert Leroy Cobb of Cobb's Galleries had been shot one morning as he was opening his shop on East 37th and Abercorn Streets in Savannah. He was in a critical condition in the hospital. A special request for prayer was asked for him. (He and his wife both graduated from Savannah Christian School). He has since made a miraculous recovery.

The fourth alumni meeting was held in the summer of 2005 for the graduates in the classes 1952-1955. This one was a low country boil held at the waterfront home of Neal and Evelyn Reagan on Burnside Island.

What a joy it has been for me to be able to attend all four of these reunions, especially this last one. Would you believe that I had not seen one of these former students in over fifty years. When I walked into the room and saw all those old people it seemed so strange. I remembered them as young people. What a difference fifty years has made in all of us.

It has been so wonderful to still take part in such wonderful trips down memory lane. They warned me that I might hear some things that I had never heard before. They still think they fooled all of us with their pranks.

There were two men there that evening who had accepted the Lord as their Savior the same day (July 10, 1948) at our Mission Youth Camp. One spent his life in the Ministry in Canada, and the other was the Music Director of his church in South Carolina.

PART FOUR

FOREIGN MISSION TRIPS

THE CALL TO BE A MISSIONARY

For my own part, I have never ceased to rejoice that God has appointed me to such an office. People talk of the sacrifice I have made in spending so much of my life in Africa. Can that be called a sacrifice, which is simply paid back as a small part of a great debt owing to our God, which we can never repay? Is that a sacrifice which brings its own best reward in healthful activity, the consciousness of doing good, peace of mind, and a bright hope of a glorious destiny hereafter?

Always with such a word, in such a view, and with such a thought! It is emphatically no sacrifice. Say rather it is a privilege. Anxiety, sickness, suffering, or danger now and then, with a foregoing of the common conveniences and charities of this life, may make us pause, and cause the spirit to waver and sink; but let this only be for a moment. All these are nothing compared with the glory which shall hereafter be revealed in and for us. I never made a sacrifice. Of this we ought not to talk when we remember the great sacrifice which He made who left His Father's throne on high, to give Himself for us.

David Livingstone

JAPAN

My husband passed away in April 1999. That Christmas I drove alone to Boca Raton, Florida to spend Christmas with my family. At that time I was blind in my left eye due to a cataract operation that destroyed my cornea. My right hand had a bad case of Carpal Tunnel Syndrome, my right ankle was in a cast and, I was facing the year 2000 alone for the first time in my life. Alas, I didn't even have a pet.

As I sat in my son's family room looking out on the water, I wondered what was left for me after being half of a couple for sixty-one years. In that condition, I poured out my heart to the Lord Jesus Christ, the only one who could help me, the one who died on the cross to save me, and the one who promised never to leave me or forsake me. I asked Him to lead me into something that would be of benefit to His Kingdom. I did not want to spend the remainder of my life here on earth as a couch potato, or rocking in a rocking chair. The remainder of this book will reveal how that particular prayer was answered.

One Sunday after church a friend asked me if I had heard about the announcement that was made in one of the Sunday School classes. I had not heard about the announcement so she told me that Joan Ackley had made the following appeal. She was planning to go on a mission trip to Japan with two other ladies, one was Nell Mason, from Mississippi, and the other lady had to drop out. If a replacement could not be found, the trip would be cancelled. I said, "Oh, I could do that. Who is Joan Ackley and how can I get in touch with her?" I called Joan that afternoon and soon I started the wheels rolling in order to get ready for the trip. I applied to Mission to the World and was accepted on the recommendations of Pastor Terry Johnson, and Bill Seymour, one of our trustees. I was then 82 years old and this was just the beginning of many wonderful opportunities for service to the

Lord. Each opportunity being quite different.

After Joan and I had been accepted to go on the trip to Japan, we were invited to a weekend conference at Simpsonwood in Atlanta, a meeting place for all men and women thinking about making a mission trip.

Joan and I quickly signed up and each sent in a check for $25.00. A few days later we received information that made us wonder if we should be going to the conference. It appeared to each of us that the weekend was planned to teach ways to raise the money for trips overseas. Since we were paying our own way to Japan, why were we going to Atlanta?

After church on Sunday we loaded our luggage in Joan's car where there were questions raised again about making the trip. We finally decided to stop in front of the Civic Center and pray about whether we should continue, or not. After praying, we decided to proceed.

When we arrived at Simpsonwood, we went to register and then to the dining hall where dinner was being served.

We were seated at a big, round table and thought we didn't know anyone, when a young lady seated across from me asked if I were Harold Deane Akins from Savannah? When I replied, "Yes." She said, "You probably don't remember me, but I went to the Mission Youth Camp with cousins in Savannah who I was visiting." She also said she accepted the Lord while at camp and was now planning to go to Kiev, Ukraine as a long-term missionary. I learned that she had been married to a former intern at the Independent Presbyterian Church, and she was the daughter-in-law of a former pastor of Eastern Heights Presbyterian Church. Since her husband's death, she had been a school teacher in Jacksonville, Florida, and was now planning to serve the Lord in the Ukraine. Our church is giving some support to her and her work.

After returning home we continued making plans for our work in Japan.

Craig Colburne was our contact in Chiba, Japan. There were constant emails back and forth. He sent a list of possible things that I could do and asked me to check the ones I felt I could do. I checked the following – I could teach either Bible or English or both. I could help in the office. I could teach crafts and help wherever I was needed. I thought he would tell me which one to prepare for, but instead, I was told to prepare for all of the above, plus prepare to teach a cooking class in the city of Nisshin-Shi, which was a part of the outreach program of the church there. Then came the email telling me to bring decorations for ten tables which would be used for a Thanksgiving Dinner. Then Mr. Colburne wanted me to receive fax messages for the third lady in our group. I told him that there were three of us going so he needed to spread some of the duties around. I felt I already had all I could handle efficiently.

The next email from him was as follows- "What would you think about sleeping on the floor?" I replied that I had never slept on the floor, but I supposed I could. I learned later that the main problem would be dressing. There was no place to sit down in order to put on hose. Joan replied that she could sleep on the floor – if someone would help her get up in the morning.

When I learned that I had the responsibility of preparing for a large cooking class, I wondered what in the world I would teach the Japanese. Everyone laughed at me when I told them I was going to teach them how to cook rice, American Style.

A few years earlier I had published a cookbook containing six hundred rice recipes. I carefully went through the book and selected one hundred recipes from which to choose my menu.

One day I had the good fortune to find a lady here at The Landings who lived in Nagoya, Japan for several years while her husband was in the service. I connected with her when I called the office to tell them that I could not accept their invitation to the gala that was planned at the Plantation Club – I would be in Japan. She then told me some things about the country and its customs. I asked her if she would be my guest for lunch and help me pick out an appropriate menu from my book, *Rice: a Food for All Seasons*. She accepted. During lunch she told me that the Japanese are very interested in important Americans. We narrowed my list to ten from which we chose: "Chicken Rice Salad," a recipe from Betty Ford, our former First Lady; "Savannah Red Rice"; and "Million Dollar Rice." Thus, we had a complete meal.

I had to prepare booklets for my cooking class. The first thing I had to do was to change the measurements to metric. As I knew absolutely nothing about that system, I had to spend the weekend learning how to make the changes.

I also had to prepare visual instructions for my crochet class in

Nisshin-Shi, as most of my pupils didn't speak English. I also had to carry yarn and crochet needles.

I was quite surprised to learn before making the trip, that Japan did not have all the products I would need. They had no canned pineapple, no Cool Whip, and other things. It is a real wonder that we passed Immigration with a box of frozen pie crusts and all the other things we were told that we should bring.

After I bought the table decorations and had them packed for shipping ahead, the day before we left, I walked down to the harbor and on my way back I noticed a lot of big, fresh pine cones. I scooped up all I could carry back home and filled all the extra spaces in my decoration box with them.

The day of departure finally came. It seemed like we had been working on our classes for months, but it had been only weeks. We left for the airport about 4:30 a.m. with Ed Hale, one of our faithful church officers as our volunteer taxi driver. When my son heard about this he said, "Mom, you didn't ask him to take you to the airport at that hour?" I replied that I did, because I sure didn't want to walk at that hour. We waited anxiously for the call to board for our flight to Atlanta where we met Nell Mason, from Mississippi, the third member of our team.

Soon we were off again. This time to Minneapolis where we waited along with 415 others to take off on our wide-bodied jet for Narita Airport in Japan.

It was daylight all the way from Savannah to Japan. We traveled with the sun going west.

Our flight took us over Alaska where the sun was shining on glaciers that looked like sparkling diamonds. Then we passed over the Aleutian Islands, and a part of Russia. The part over Russia was something new – permission to fly that route was recently given.

When I stepped off the plane at Narita Airport in Chiba, I immediately noticed the completely blank, expressionless faces of the Japanese. Seldom did we see one smiling, but I also noticed the cleanliness of their cities and buildings.

I was soon introduced to the custom of taking off my shoes upon entering a home, slipping on the slippers provided, and of changing that pair of slippers for another pair upon going into the powder room. This was all reversed upon leaving.

The Japanese have a custom of giving gifts every time they visit a friend. We were warned before leaving home to take plenty of gifts.

We stayed in the home of missionaries who were on furlough, and were not prepared for the cold weather we were experiencing. We slept upstairs and the two-burner oil heater was in the living room downstairs. We made out very well until shower time. They do not have hot water tanks like we have. The water is heated while showering, so that was all a new experience. After all, we were missionaries – and not staying at the Hilton.

We were treated to a day in Tokyo where we went to a Kabuki-Za Theatre show, an all male show. The men were dressed like women and they really put on a show. It was all done in Japanese, but booklets, or tapes, could be purchased so that we could follow the spoken lines.

Next we went to a grocery store. The meat and seafood sections went half the way around the huge building. We didn't recognize many cuts of meat or seafood. They have so much more seafood than we have here. They had a special section for cuts of eel, a favorite delicacy among the Japanese.

Our guide on one of our day tours was a long-term missionary, who knew what we would enjoy seeing. He took us to see two different types of shrines. After seeing rice fields and some of the modern buildings in Tokyo, we then went to a Buddhist Shrine which was having a "3-5-7 Day" – which meant that all little girls of those ages were dressed in full Japanese dress. They wore bright colored kimonos, silk slippers, and had hairdos like adults. That was where we did most of our shopping, as there were endless booths selling mostly Japanese style goods.

One of the missionary couples, both of them are ophthalmologists, invited us to their home for lunch where we enjoyed our first Korean Pears, a Japanese salad that I can't name, and other Japanese dishes. It was inspiring to sit and talk with them about the work they are doing. Their children are attending school there, and they feel that it is an opportunity they will never regret.

It was then time to go to work. We had a thorough orientation with Dan Iverson, who heads the work in Chiba. He pointed out the dos and don'ts that should be observed in a foreign country. We then started our assignments which included participating in English and Bible classes.

In Chiba, my crochet class was made up of daughters of American Missionaries. Joan, who also crochets, helped me with the classes. When I saw the Iverson girls at the Missionary Conference in Atlanta, they told me that they are still crocheting, and had made all their Christmas gifts. After I returned to Savannah from Chiba, I picked out some crochet books that I thought a beginning teenager would enjoy using, and sent them to the girls by a man from Mission to the World.

While we were in Chiba, Nell Mason received word that her sister had died – so she left us and returned home.

It was now time to move on. This time a ride on the famous bullet train to Nagoya where we were picked up for our trip to Nisshin-Shi. I had seen pictures of their famous trains on television and I realized they were traveling like bullets, but to experience it is quite different. A gauge at the front of the car tells the speed the train is traveling. When it registered one hundred twenty-five, I really hoped we wouldn't meet a train coming down the same track the wrong way.

While working in Nisshin-Shi, I stayed with Cynthia Ruble, a young school teacher from the United States. Next I had the privilege of staying in the Ogasawara home with Takeo and his wife Reiko. The evening I arrived at their home, Reiko told Takeo to go show me how to operate the toilet and she would show me about the shower and hot tub later. When Takeo showed me how all the buttons worked, I felt more confident to use the facilities. Later that evening Reiko showed me where and how to shower, then how to lift the cover to the hot tub and soak after I had already showered. I was not to let the water out of the tub. Everyone else would use the same water.

I especially cherish the memory of the good times I had with Cynthia and the Ogasawaras. Takeo and Reiko took Cynthia and me to a Chinese restaurant where we enjoyed an authentic Chinese meal. I later welcomed Tomohito Ogasawara, their son, to my home for a visit.

In Nisshin, the missionaries had planned to have a big Thanksgiving dinner and sold about seventy-five tickets, however, over one hundred showed up for the traditional American Thanksgiving dinner with turkey, and all the trimmings. Joan and I baked pumpkin pies all afternoon. It was interesting to see the young ladies put cranberry sauce on their pumpkin pie.

The tables were decorated with the colorful tablecloths, green and orange candles, turkeys, pumpkins, and the cornucopias I shipped over, including the pine cones.

The missionaries had prepared a full American style Thanksgiving dinner. Ladies brought covered dishes. Several of the Japanese ladies brought dishes of their specialties just for me – eel.

After the Thanksgiving dinner was over and we were cleaning up, I noticed every decoration that I had bought was still there on the tables, but every pine cone was gone. The guests had taken every one of them.

After dinner the teachers put on an American Play.

My crochet class in Nisshin-Shi was one of the most delightful crochet classes I ever had. It was a class of boys and girls about eight to twelve years of age. One little Japanese boy caught on right away, and was making several lines of crocheting, when he motioned for me to come over to him. He told me that he wanted to make a blanket for his little plastic donkey and asked if I would help him. I assured him that I would not leave until we finished the blanket. We did finish the blanket, and one happy boy left with his donkey and the blanket. The next morning he came back quite enthused with his new-found skill. He told his teacher that he was going to crochet a scarf for himself.

What a thrill it was to share my knowledge of crocheting with so many in that far away land. This was fun, but the biggest thrill I had was my cooking class in that city.

Mrs. Wayne Newsome, a long-term missionary, who spoke Japanese better than I speak English, was my able interpreter and helper. She and I prepared a lot of the ingredients at her home the day before. We were to cook the meal in a classroom with only chairs, a table, and a piano, but no cooking equipment. We had to carry everything, including our Microwave, to the second floor.

I was thrilled when they told me that was the largest turnout they ever had. I think they were curious about an American coming to teach them how to cook rice. There were many men present which was a surprise. They called me a "celebrity".

After we had finished cooking the meal and the plates had been served, two well-dressed young Japanese business women motioned for me to go over to them. They handed me their business cards, and at once started asking me many questions. The first was,

"How old are you?" I told them. Then they asked, "Who paid for your trip?" When I told them that I did, they then asked, "Why did you leave your home thousands of miles away and come here to Japan?" I replied, "I have come to tell you about a living Savior." The Japanese have two gods – Buddha and Shinto, but neither is a living god.

We had emailed our testimonies to Craig before we left Savannah so they could be translated and read in the different services.

One special comment I want to make before leaving my report on Japan. Joan and I could walk anywhere – day or night alone, and be perfectly safe.

How I wish that could be said of Savannah.

One thing special I learned in Japan is that the missionaries really look forward even to short-term visits by missionaries. It gives them encouragement in their work. They know that people back home really care about what they are doing for the Lord on the foreign field. After such a wonderful time, it was hard to say, "Goodbye," and head back to Savannah.

Nell and I With Missionaries

Sunday Night Service in a Home With Tokuhiro Meiri

Sacred Tatomi Room

The Ogasawaras
Takeo, Tomohito, Reiko

Craig Colburn, Our Coodinator
and the Three Old Ladies

Crochet Class in Chiba

Long-Term Missionaries
Rev. and Mrs. Wayne Newsome and Children

Our English Class

Wendy and I Around Heater

Toilet

RICE: A FOOD FOR ALL SEASONS

Psalms 104:14. He causeth the grass to grow for the cattle, and herb for the service of man: that he may bring forth food out of the earth.

In 1989, I published a cookbook entitled *Rice: A Food for All Seasons*. It was a collection of 600 Favorite Rice Recipes. I drew from this book for my cooking class in Japan.

I have always liked to cook, and being a Southerner, rice was nearly always a staple in our meals. I collected rice recipes for over thirty years and worked with the Rice Council and Riviana Foods, both of Houston, Texas.

I wrote to many famous people asking for their favorite rice recipes. I shall never forget my excitement when George, Sr. called me from the front door one day and said, "Come here," The White House is on the phone and wants to talk with you."

I had a very pleasant talk with Assistant Usher Christopher B. Emery, Executive Residence, The White House. He sent a copy of the menu for a State dinner held on April 19th honoring their Majesties the King and Queen of Jordan. This was one of the most formal dinners under the first Bush presidency. There were 117 guests seated at twelve round tables in the State Dining Room. Rice was served with the main course. I was also told that some form of rice is served at nearly all State dinners.

In my research, I learned so many things about rice. Rice came to South Carolina quite by accident. Today rice is grown in several states. Seeds are sown from airplanes, and harvesting is done by machinery. There are as many as 7,000 different types of rice.

TAIWAN

Psalms 51:12-13. Restore unto me the joy of thy salvation; and uphold me with thy free spirit. Then will I teach transgressors thy ways; and sinners shall be converted unto thee.

Soon Joan and I were off again. This time to Taipei, Taiwan on a very different missionary journey – having a part in the American Village at Christ's College. Students signed up for a three-hour course of study about America. They attended classes mornings and afternoons, and the evenings were spent in special programs of entertainment. One of the features was a banquet where the young men served the tables. Later when we asked the girls what they liked most about the banquet - they replied in unison, "The young men waiting the tables."

For the missionaries, the days started with Bible reading and prayer. Then we were off to our duties. I was asked to help prepare breakfast. Each morning I was to peel and cut up the most wonderful Mangoes I have ever seen or tasted. Were they ever delicious. Joan helped with the dish washing. Lunch was catered each day at noon by a different Chinese restaurant. They served many dishes that I was not familiar with, but for the most part they were very good. I haven't acquired a taste for seaweed, and some of their other specialties.

Someone had donated bolts of cloth to the college to be used for tablecloths. Joan and I rounded up two sewing machines and started cutting and hemming tablecloths. They really added a lot to our banquet.

Joan and I were asked to prepare the mashed potatoes for the banquet. Off we went to one of the houses on campus to prepare our assigned dish. It was agreed that I was to peel all the potatoes and Joan was to take care of the cooking. Everything was moving along wonderfully well for two novices. When we finished the cooking process and it was time to mash the potatoes we saw the huge restaurant-style machine - all closed up. We almost panicked. Of course, there was no one to ask and no manual could be located so we tried the old trial-and-error method. With much help from, and dependence upon the Lord, we finished just as two young men came to take them over to the banquet room.

One afternoon we had a cookout where hamburgers and hot dogs were grilled. Many of the games that American young people enjoy were played – like sack races, relays, Simon Says, and dodge ball.

The greatest privilege that each of us had was living in the dormitory with four young Chinese students. We had devotions with them and each evening we used one of the "I ams" of the book of John to explain that Jesus is The Light of the World, The Bread of Life, The Door, The Good Shepherd, The Resurrection and The Life, and The True Vine. In my dorm room there were two professing Christians and two Buddhists. At the close of the week, three Chinese girls accepted Christ and two of them were in my room. Praise the Lord. Many of them were strengthened in the Lord. It is so hard for them to come out from the faith their families embrace.

The American Village Experience was wonderfully arranged. The students began by planning a trip to the United States, securing a passport, buying a ticket, and boarding a make-believe plane set up on one side of an auditorium. The course carried them through each phase of the trip until arriving in classes. It was so wonderful to see all of them studying about our wonderful country.

In one of the game sessions, I won a tea set, which led to my meeting the president of the Tea Club and a wonderful demonstration of how to really make tea. Barbara White and I enjoyed an hour with him in his home where we saw his collection of tea pots and books. Before leaving, he gave me some green tea. He also showed us a tea cake, that looked like a one-layer, round cake only the color of tea. He said the sale of that *one* cake of tea would pay for his son's education.

Before I went to Taipei, a friend told me to be sure to go to the Grand Hotel. It is a magnificent, famous hotel where the Shah of Iran stayed when he visited Taipei. We not only went to the hotel, but our friend Barbara White took us there for lunch. This hotel was formerly a palace of the Empress, and was converted to a hotel.

The lobby floor and the wide-stairway leading to the mezzanine floor are constructed of marvelous white marble. In back of the hotel there are luscious green hills that make a beautiful background for the hotel. The round red columns make the entrance very bright and colorful. The memorial park to Chiang Kai-shek is nearby.

Then we went across the street and shopped in a three-story building that sold so many gifts, it was hard to decide what to buy.

Another day Joan and I went to the famous museum there. It is equally as wonderful as the one my family and I visited in Cairo, Egypt, where King Tutankhamen's great collection is located.

One evening we were all treated to a trip to town to a large shopping center where we all went shopping and visited Starbuck's for a cup of their coffee.

One afternoon, Barbara arranged for me to be photographed and interviewed by a news reporter. I asked the reporter if she would give me a copy of the report when it was finished. She said that she would be happy to give me a copy, but it would be in Chinese.

Taipei is a city located at the foot of beautiful mountains and surrounded by water. Unfortunately, it is subject to typhoons. We experienced one while we were there, and another one was due right after we left. They are different from our hurricanes here, but nevertheless, frightening.

A young Chinese lady at the college had saved her money for a good while, in order to give each missionary a beautiful silk embroidery piece with birds which I had framed and have on the wall of my living room.

I still get emails from some of the young people with whom I shared a delightful period of time. God bless them. I shall never forget them. They are very dear to my heart.

——— My Dorm Girls and Me ———

Barbara White and Me
in the Grand Hotel

American Village
the Whole Group, Faculty and Students

Inside Grand Hotel in Taipei

Faculty and Missionaries

KENYA AND KIBERA 2003

II Corinthians 6:10. "As sorrowful, yet always rejoicing: as poor, yet making many rich; as having nothing, and yet possessing all things."

When I told my son I was planning to go on a World Mission journey to Kenya to work with abandoned street children and children in an orphanage. He said, "Mom, go anywhere but not to Kenya."

I asked, "Why?"

He said. "Haven't you heard about the bombing of our embassy there?"

I said, "Yes, I have."

"What about the attempt to shoot down an El Al plane there?"

I said that I was aware of that.

He said, "And you are still going?"

My reply was "Yes." End of conversation.

Joan Ackley and I had already had two fantastic missionary trips – Japan and Taiwan, but she said, "No" to Kenya. Therefore, I left alone headed for Detroit where I was to meet the nine others who were making the trip to Nairobi.

The first news I received upon boarding in Savannah was there would be no restroom facilities until we reached Detroit, because needed repairs to the restroom facilities could not be made in Savannah.

I spent a long, lonely day at the airport in Detroit. I watched the news on TV, and recall that day we had one of the best stock market rallies in a good while.

Late in the afternoon, I met the nine others and even though they were complete strangers up to that moment, we all immediately bonded with a common goal – to do all we could to help those people in Kenya. We soon started on one of the greatest experiences of my life. There were six medical missionaries, one guide, and three of us "flunkies." Of course, I fell into that category. What Christ-like, dedicated missionaries they were. A newly wed doctor and her husband were a great asset to our group.

We soon boarded for our flight to Amsterdam. After we fastened our seat belts for take-off, this announcement came on the intercom. Our compass wasn't working, and we couldn't leave until it was repaired. After the repairs were made, we took off.

My first trip across the Atlantic was in 1957. It took nine days on our ship, the Italia. This is my ninth crossing and it was to take nine hours. It was by far the most spectacular. There was a beautiful full moon shining on the white cloud cover and the water. It was breathtaking. I felt a person hasn't really lived until they have had an experience like that. How marvelous is God's handiwork.

We flew over Scotland. Early the next morning we arrived in Amsterdam where we spent most of the day. We finally took off on the last leg of our flight to Nairobi, Kenya. As we flew over the Sahara Desert, many passengers came over to my side of the plane to get a better view. After flying all day, we arrived at our destination.

Ah, Nairobi – the birthplace of Roger Whitaker, famous British singer and songwriter, and the city of contrasts – wealth and poverty. Hundreds of men were sitting along the curbs, or were aimlessly walking about. Men and women are seldom seen walking together in Nairobi.

Although it was very hot, and we had no air conditioning in our van, we had to ride through Nairobi with all windows closed and locked with no purses, or cameras in view from the outside. When cars stopped for traffic lights, men would surround the vehicles looking for something to steal. They would even break windows if there was something inside they saw and could quickly grab.

There was an estimated 60,000 children living on the streets of that great city. Many were born there, and had lived all their lives there.

The average life span was forty-seven years and the average pay for those lucky enough to have a job was $1.00 per day.

We arrived in Nairobi late Saturday night and early Sunday morning we were off to church in a nine-passenger van with about fifteen passengers.

What a glorious service we had in that little building. The singing was wonderful. They sang the good old gospel hymns like "Rock of Ages" in Swahili and we in English. A young lady beat out the rhythm on a big drum.

When that little preacher began to pray and thank God for *all* of His blessings. I sat there comparing my blessings to his blessings, and I wondered how he could move us so deeply. Of course, I wondered for a moment what blessings he had. Then the reason became very clear – he said that when we have Jesus, we have *everything*. Praise the Lord. How right he was.

I will never forget the blessing I received that morning. Oh, if the Christians here would stop and think of all the blessings we have here in America.

Outside the building the grounds were covered with trash and garbage. I asked the minister why they didn't have a clean-up day and make the place look better. Since most of that beautiful, large modern city of Nairobi, and all the country-side was like that, they didn't even notice it.

Our trip to Kenya was divided mainly into two parts – Kajiado, where between seventy-five and one hundred Maasai orphans are cared for and educated through the efforts especially of the Rupps from North Carolina. That, too, was an unforgettable experience.

The contrast between the clothing and toys of the average American child and the Kajiado orphanage children is immense. For example, the American child plays with remote-controlled robots, video games, and elaborately dressed dolls. I saw a Kajiado child playing with a bent stick to which was attached a canning jar lid. He pushed his toy around all afternoon. Some of our team taught them how to play hopscotch that was scratched into the ground with a stick.

Rita Hill, my "roomie" and I enjoyed sitting out under the trees and talking with the children. They enjoyed feeling and platting our hair, also pulling my hose out from my legs and letting them go. I was called upon to teach a class of boys and girls. They came to the appointed room without books, paper, or pencils. Since this was to be an arithmetic class, I hurriedly grabbed my notebook and began writing down some simple arithmetic problems of addition and subtraction. One little girl added all the addition ones correctly, but evidently not knowing anything about subtraction – she changed the subtraction sign to a plus sign and then added them. That's an unusual way to solve a problem I would say.

I gave them paper and a few crayons and asked them to draw

some pictures for me. They drew church buildings and what they called pictures of themselves. The pictures were quite revealing. Keep in mind, their language was Swahili and we had to resort to an improvised sign language in order to communicate. I also had meetings with the teachers.

One of the delights of our stay there was the Chai, a tea that was served to us each morning. We were told before we got there that our meals would be as follows: rice and beans every day for lunch and cabbage and whatever other green vegetables were available for the evening meals. We were also told we must not throw out anything. So be sure not to take out more than we expected to eat.

We ate in the dining room with the children. Their plates were served first in the tiny kitchen and when all the plates were served they were brought out into the dining hall. While the preparation of the plates was taking place, the flies were swarming all over the food. I asked the Mission to the World leader, who was traveling with us, if I gave the money for window screens could I be assured the money would be spent for that purpose. She said that they couldn't promise that because if the children needed food more than the screens they would get the food.

In the 1960s I had traveled on a missionary trip through Mexico and Guatemala where I saw much poverty. My family and I later toured Israel and Egypt. Outside Cairo, we saw a graveyard where people were living. They leaned cardboard boxes on tombstones for shelter and ate from the nearby garbage cans. We wondered how even animals could live in such a place. We were there in September and it had not rained that year. Dust covered everything. A bus passed us not only covered with dust, but there were so many people hanging onto the outside of the bus – I said, "That bus is really loaded." Our guide replied, "It is not full – as long as you can still see parts of the bus."

However even after seeing the extreme poverty in Mexico, Guatemala, and Egypt, I was not prepared for what I saw in Kenya, particularly in Kibera.

Kibera is next to the largest slum in the world. Between 700,000 and a million people live there in cow dung huts with no electricity, ventilation, running water, or bath facilities, and no roads, sidewalks, or even paths – just the sides of the ditches that serve as the disposal for all the wastes.

Martha and Imbumi Makuku

The Mission to the World work in Kibera is headed by Imbumi Makuku, a native of Kenya who accepted the Lord, came to Orlando on a scholarship and graduated from the Reformed Theological Seminary. He surprised everyone by going back to work in the slum in Kibera. Some even suggested that if he lived in this country, he, his wife, and sons would have a better life, but he said the Lord had called him to Kibera, so he must go there. Martha, his wife, who is a nurse, works with him.

My first visit to this slum was with Imbumi and a few of our group. After he got a key and let us into the building, he said that he wanted to give us his vision for this building standing in the middle of this slum. He said that four rooms could be rented for $50 per month, and he believed that if he got started with the four he would be able to rent more of the rooms as the work grew. He called on me to lead in prayer. After praying, I told Imbumi that I would give him $200 right there for the first four months, and that I would be responsible for one year's rent. I would either give it myself, or get some friends to help.

We soon bid our friends in Nairobi, "*Adieu*," and headed for the airport for the flight home. We taxied out on the field at midnight, only to hear the following message on the intercom "One engine is not responding. We will have to go back to the terminal for repairs." After a delay, we finally arrived home safely.

Shortly after renting the four rooms and beginning a pre-school program, a small clinic, a youth work, and regular church services, Imbumi was notified that the building was up for sale and would be sold promptly. Wallace Anderson from Mission to the World, called me immediately and we were both devastated.

We didn't know what we could do.

The next day I was going over my portfolio, and to my amazement a stock that I had bought in 1997 at $17 per share had appreciated to the exact amount needed to buy that building. I called Chloe Dekle, my stock broker at Merrill Lynch, and told her to transfer the stock to Mission to the World so they could purchase the building. There were many things that added to the cost – the rate of exchange, all the legal work, etc; however, the Lord wonderfully provided. Imbumi said he had faith the Lord would supply the funds, but didn't know it would come the way it did.

It is not necessary for me to say – Kibera is where my heart was so deeply touched, and where we now have the Kibera Reformed Presbyterian Church. May it always be a refuge of hope for those people who have such little hope as AIDS is very prevalent there.

When we were in Kenya, we were told that there were no public schools for children. However, there is new hope for all of Kenya now since the election in December 2002. After a president who served for 24 years, there is a new president.

My Second Trip To Kenya – 2004

Before I left Kenya, I promised that whenever he had the dedication of the building, I would return. The next year George Jr. went with me to the celebration. I told him that some of his inheritance went for the building, so it was partly from him.

At the time I told him I wanted him to go with me to the dedication of the building, I didn't stop to realize what I was asking of him. He had to get a visa, he had to take Larium for two weeks before the trip, during the trip, and two weeks after returning. Larium is an antimalarial medication that can have serious side effects in some people. In addition, George, Jr. had to leave his business and fly tourist class, as all Mission to the World missionaries do, and walk through Kibera on a very hot day to get to the building.

He did have a few amenities. He hired a private driver and a van to take him on a Safari, to a Maasai camp, to tour Nairobi, the Rift Valley, and many other places.

I want him to know how much I appreciate his sacrifice for me. He truly is a Special Son.

About two hundred people attended the Dedication program. Most of them were teenagers singing gospel hymns and choruses. There were testimonies and messages given.

As I stood there looking up to Heaven with tears of joy streaming down my cheeks, I said, "Lord, how I thank you for giving me the opportunity of providing this building for this work."

When I attended a prayer meeting for mothers with AIDS, it was heart breaking to hear them say, "When I die (not if I die), who will take care of my children?"

When we go on these missionary trips we do have an opportunity to go sight-seeing. Our group went to Amboseli Park, within view of Kilimanjaro. We rode in vans with open tops so we could see the animals. When we stopped for a rest stop in the park, we were quickly surrounded with eager little monkeys. Rita Hill put her bag in front of the van when we went inside. While we were in the building, the monkeys got in her bag and ate her lunch. Naughty, naughty little rascals.

We went to the famous Rift Valley and to Karen, where part of the movie, "Out of Africa" was filmed. We had a delicious meal in the famous house there. We went to the markets, visited several churches, etc.

Imbumi and, his wife Martha visited me last year along with Opal Hardgrove from Mission to the World. I look forward to their return, and I still have not given up hope of another trip to Kenya.

Roger Whitaker once said that no one leaves Africa without taking a part of it in their hearts. He also said that Africa is never quiet. He was right. When we were in bed at night we could always hear the animals in the distance.

As George, Jr. and I were heading for the airport in Nairobi for our trip home, there was the most beautiful rainbow in the sky I had ever seen. The colors were vibrant, This reminded me of the following quote by William Wordsworth:

"My heart leaps when I behold a rainbow in the sky."

I can truthfully say that my trips to Kenya changed my life forever in many positive ways.

KIBERA

The following is reprinted from a *Mission To The World* report on Kibera:

> The Kibera slum began in 1912 when retired Sudanese Nubian soldiers from the British Kings African Rifles were allocated land in the area. They must have served 12 years in the army to qualify. The Nubians are now in their eighth generation. They are mostly Muslims and have kept their culture intact.
>
> Over the years other tribal groups began to settle in the area either renting from the Nubians or by being allocated land to build on a temporary basis by the government. In most cases money changes hands before one is given a plot to build on. Kibera is close to the city center and to the industries so most people can walk to work. It is a reservoir of very cheap labor for the city.
>
> It is estimated that right now 700,000-1.2 million people live there. Over 83% of the population are underemployed or unemployed. Most make $1 per day. That goes to fend for 4.2 people in the small 10x10 room that they rent. 54% of Kenya makes $1 a day.
>
> Kibera is divided into 10 areas – most of the neighborhoods based on tribe. The Nubians still look at themselves as the rightful owners of the slum and thus they have resisted physically attempts by other tribes to encroach on their supremacy. This resulted in November 2001 in over ten people losing their lives when clashes broke out over the issue of the tenants paying cheaper rent. The tension still simmers under the surface.

George, Jr., Imbumi, Me With Two Interns

Kibera

Slum

The Sign to Our Building

Inside the Building in Kibera

The Orphanage, Kajiado

Children at Kajiado With Me

More Children

Outdoor Bathroom. Behind the Masai Cloth: Gina (L),
Marty (R). Charysoe holding cloth (L) covering her face

My Room at the Kenyan "Ritz"

Lunch on the Safari

Entrance to Amboseli National Park

Elephants

Nairobi

Ethiopian Restaurant in Nairobi

Going to Church

Traveling Through Town

Dedication

Dedication

HAITI

Acts 9:39 Tabitha (Dorcas). And all the widows stood by him weeping and showing the coats and garments Dorcas made, while she was with them.

Before I made my second mission trip to Nairobi, Ann Mercer Klein called me one day and asked me if I would consider going to Haiti to teach the ladies to sew. I told her that I would put her request on the back burner and pray about going there after I returned from Kenya.

Later that summer, I attended a trunk show at Sew Much More in Garden City, Georgia. One of the teachers from Pfaff, the Germany-based sewing machine manufacturer, was giving demonstrations on the new machines and told of her interest in teaching young people to sew. She had bought six sewing machines, set them up in her basement and had young boys and girls come to sewing lessons. Right then I began thinking about buying six machines, getting together a group of ladies to help teach, and plan for a fall trip to Haiti.

I talked with Ann about it, and she informed me that we would need an interpreter - as the Haitians speak Creole. She would provide one for us in Haiti. I then thought about asking one of the Pfaff teachers to go with us. I first thought of the lady who told us about her classes in her basement, but the Lord definitely directed me to call the other one - not knowing that she was born in France, had lived in the Dominican Republic, and spoke French and Creole. How wonderfully our dear Lord leads us along.

When I called Nadine Scott about going with us, her reply was, "When do we leave?" The Pfaff company agreed to pay her expenses and donated many supplies for the classes.

Bonnie and Jim Brooks, who own and operate Sew Much More joined with us and contributed toward our trip in so many ways. Bonnie made the trip with us. She encouraged her customers to contribute cash, or material, for the classes.

Independent Presbyterian Church loaned us a bus and Jim drove us to the hotel near the airport in Jacksonville and met us in Jacksonville for the return trip to Savannah.

The following contributors had a part in the purchase of six sewing machines and two sergers: Independent Presbyterian Church, Rose McRae, Sonja Byrd, Jerry Sammons, and Harold Deane Akins.

Our group was composed of the following: Joan Ackley, Bonnie Brooks, Joan Kornblatt, Nadine Scott, Harold Deane Akins, and Jeff Klein. No, Jeff did not go to teach sewing. He went to do construction work.

We spent the first night of our trip at the Red Roof Inn in Jacksonville. We had an early curfew, as there was a call in for a taxi to pick us up at 6 a.m. to go to the airport. After a breakfast, and some usual waiting, we lined up for boarding, but nothing was happening. Soon the announcement came that the flight to Miami was cancelled. The next flight would be an afternoon one, and, of course, we would miss the flight out of Miami to Port-au-Prince. An overnight stop in Miami was not in our plans. But such is the joy of traveling. Be prepared for the inevitable at all times. Traveling is not for the faint-hearted.

The next morning, upon arriving at the airport, Jeff got all our luggage, which was ten or eleven duffle bags of cloth and machines. An employee at the airport ordered Jeff over to our left and yelled, "All of you wives, go to the right." From then on, we gave our "husband, Jeff," a hard time. We wondered what Ann would think of him and his Harem?

When we arrived in Haiti, we were led quickly to our vehicle where we traveled with an armed guard.

Soon we arrived at the compound in Messalier which was about forty-five miles from the capital city.

We all roomed in the same building. Jeff was on the other side of the wall, and we knew that he liked to read at night - but we all enjoyed annoying him. We sang every song we knew at the top of our voices - even a good bit off key.

Each morning around four or four thirty a.m. the rooster, on the other side of the wall, gave us the wake-up call. It was so hot in the early part of the night we didn't get to sleep until late, and were not happy with said rooster.

Although the accommodations were adequate - it was not the

Ritz. Some even dared to think the food was the pits. We were sure of water - hot water to drink and cold water for showers. We were living like real missionaries.

Our teaching experience was about to begin. We had high hopes. Perhaps we might find at least one Dorcas who would be able to carry on after we left. We were expecting six students for each sewing class. We were somewhat overwhelmed when about twenty showed up for each class. We found two that were able to continue what we had begun, Elvena, an elderly lady with some commercial sewing experience, and Felix, a male teenager.

We were all packed in a windowless room with a small fan that worked occasionally. We can appreciate the news about the sweat shops around the world. We experienced one first-hand.

Praise the Lord. What a rewarding experience this was. It was worth all the effort that we put forth to make it all happen.

We all looked forward to the big trip we were promised to a beautiful resort, not too far away, where we could go shopping, swimming, eat a good meal, and enjoy the beautiful scenery. That was the weekend getaway. We sang all the way, rode over some of the biggest potholes in the world, and most of us didn't eat any of the food - Nadine identified the meat on the table as cat.

The "shopping" was two men with a few paintings and gifts that they had laid out on the grass. After all, we were in the poorest country in the Western Hemisphere, weren't we?

All things end – some good, but some sad. I, for one, have really been sad when we had to leave one of our missionary projects - and this was no exception. It is like leaving our own family permanently. We may never see those pupils again.

We flew most of the day, and landed back in Jacksonville, where Jim came to pick us up. Savannah looked good, even at midnight.

Nadine Scott From Pfaff With Student

Bonnie With Our Dorcas

Shower Time

The Finished Product

The Team
Joan Kornblatt, Bonnie Brooks, Nadine Scott, Joan Ackley, and Me

Our Weekend Getaway

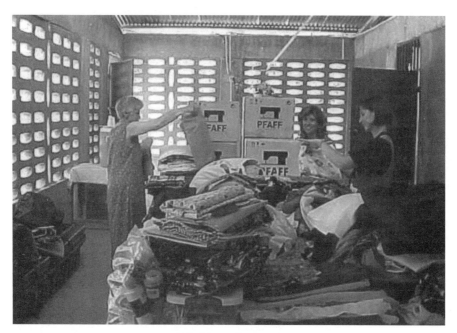

We Have Arrived

The Compound

Charles Amicy's House

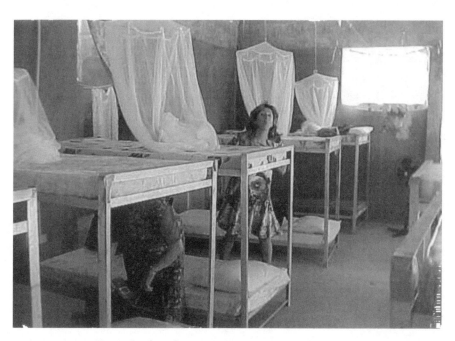

Our Beds at the Haiti "Ritz"

All Packed Up

Sergers Are Ready

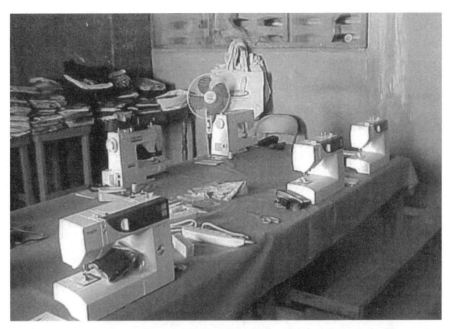

Fan, Machines, and Fabrics are Ready

Sewing Classes Begin

PART FIVE

LATER ON

HAROLD DEANE AKINS

HAS BEEN LISTED

AS A

MEMBER

IN THE

GLOBAL REGISTER'S

WHO'S WHO

IN

EXECUTIVES AND PROFESSIONALS

2006 – 2007
EDITION

ALASKA

Colossians 1:16. For by him were all things created, that are in heaven, and that are in earth, visible and invisible, whether they be thrones, or dominions, or principalities, or powers: all things were created by him, and for him.

Between my last two trips to Africa, my sister-in-law Phyllis Griffith, her daughter, Linda Griffith, and I took a delightful trip to Alaska.

Phyllis has two sisters who are residents of Ketchikan, Alaska where they are high school teachers. One husband is a teacher in the university and the other owns a bottling company. Ketchikan is the salmon and fishing capitol of Alaska.

When our ship docked, the sisters met us and took us for a special day of sightseeing, shopping, going right down to a glacier, and for an Alaskan lunch. We visited the homes of the sisters, met the children and the dogs. When I was growing up, I thought that Alaskans lived in igloos. Instead, they were living in modern homes by the wide Alaskan rivers. Our day there was a get-together that was something like a family reunion and most enjoyable.

After leaving Ketchikan, we went panning for gold. Each of us panned enough for some jewelry of which we were very proud. We also went to Denali National Park and Preserve, and saw several shows by the natives.

I was surprised to see so many beautiful flowers all over Alaska so early in the spring. The weather was also very nice, cool, but not cold.

Since we took the trip that went all the way to Fairbanks, we had a long train ride in the observation car before we met the ship.

We saw a stretch of the famous pipe line. Other places we visited were - Juneau, Alaska's capitol city, and Anchorage. At each stop we mostly shopped and saw a few places of historical interest.

A nice part of the trip was an afternoon cruise aboard the Sternwheeler Discovery, offering other sights and places to explore.

We visited a native village, met an Iditarod champion and her sled dogs, and watched a bush-pilot demonstration.

The highlight of that evening was a Welcome Salmon Bake at Alaska Land, for some good eating of fish and poultry.

Our ship took us through the Inside Passage, with its pristine water and snow-capped mountains, and finally to Vancouver, British Columbia. The Vancouver market was quite large with many good eating places. We had to wait a long time for our lunch as all the passengers were eating there.

Our last stop was Seattle where we were treated to a tour of the High Technology Corridor (Silicon Valley) and other places of interest. We spent the last night of our tour there before boarding our plane for old Savannah which required a stopover in Chicago.

Before we arrived at O'Hare Airport in Chicago, our tour guide called for a wheelchair for an elderly lady on our tour who was unable to walk. There was a breakdown in communication and when we arrived at the airport there was a long line of wheelchairs waiting for us. We decided rather than waste their efforts we would all be wheeled to the next concourse. We were quite a spectacle as we went through the airport whooping and hollering in our wheelchairs.

Close to a Glacier

Panning For Gold

Pipeline

Garden Scene

Show At Denali

Lady and Her Iditarod Dogs

WHY ME?

Psalms 116:12. What shall I render unto the Lord for all his benefits toward me?

Why me? That is a question we often ask when something we think is bad happens to us – but I am using it in juxtaposition – why have so many wonderful things happened to me?

When I was sitting in the den at George, Jr.'s house and wondering if all the good things were over, I made a decision. I was not going to let loneliness and inactivity rule my life. Not me.

With the Lord's Guidance and Help I was going to live the best years of my life – the ones that were still ahead of me, even if I am an octogenarian. As I take a look back over these nearly seven years, I can truthfully say they have truly been glorious, wonderful years. I haven't had time to be lonely or unhappy. Who said that widowhood was a lonely, sad time? Many widows, and widowers, give up and hope they will soon join their departed mates.

I have missed my mate of sixty-one years. We had a great life together and I have missed his smile, and his loving touch. For several years I watched him get sicker, and we both knew at ninety-one there wasn't much hope. When he started looking up toward Heaven and asking, "Lord, why don't you take me?" George, Jr. and I agreed that we wouldn't spend any long time grieving because we knew George, Sr. was happier where he is now.

The one sad time I had was when I went to Boca Raton, Florida for the first Christmas without George, Sr. He had always given a Bible message to the family after the Christmas dinner. They asked me to take his place that year. That was one of the hardest things I had to do. I couldn't keep the tears from falling, no matter how hard I tried. I wanted to be the strong one, but I failed.

When men and women retire at a young age, there are so many years left that they can use their resources of time and money for good. That brings more joy than any worldly pleasure or treasure. I would like to challenge some of you, to take a foreign mission trip and use your God given talents and money to help those hungry, sick people, who can't help themselves.

You'll be very glad you did.

FINAL THOUGHTS

Isaiah 14:24. The Lord of hosts hath sworn, saying, Surely as I have thought, so shall it come to pass; and as I have purposed, so shall it stand.

Has This Child Fulfilled the Dream and Prayer the Father Had For It?

Whatever I was To Be, I Have Now Become.

As I come to the conclusion of my memoirs, you may ask, "Any regrets?" Yes, of course, I have some – but I don't want them to blot out the joys and the accomplishments.

Lee Iococca, a former president of the Chrysler Corporation, once said, "It is not what you leave behind, but what you started."

It is also not what life throws at you, but how you handle it.

There are only 24 hours in a day. Everyone has the same number of hours. It's how you choose to use them. Once used, they are gone forever.

Be careful of how you live – Robert Murray McCheyne, the renowned Scottish preacher, said, "Live so you will be remembered."

As I read the accomplishments and failures of the men and women of the Bible and stop to look within – "What have I done with my life?"

I often wonder if my earthly father would be pleased with me – if I have become the Christian he prayed I would become, but I also face the more important question "Is my Heavenly Father pleased with me as one of His children?"

The question gives us all cause for thought. When I go to Heaven, will both of my fathers be able to say, "Well done – welcome home, my child."

My prayer for you is that your life will be worth imitating.

Remember, you are more powerful on your knees.

Captain Al Naismith
and Harold Deane Akins

Hey, Isn't It Time to Eat?

Zell Miller and Me

Governor Sonny Perdue,
Al Naismith, and Me

Liz James and Me
The Day We Sold Our Property

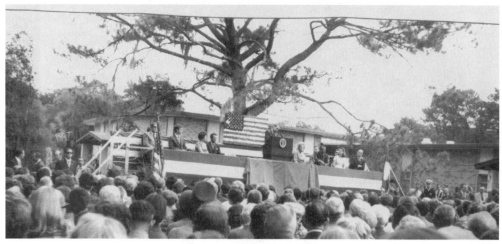

President and Mrs. Nixon,
Julie and David at Skidaway

AFTER THOUGHTS

Psalms 119:105. Thy word is a lamp unto my feet, and a light unto my path.

Titus 3:5. Not by works of righteousness which we have done, but according to his mercy he saved us, by the washing of regeneration, and renewing of the Holy Ghost.

MY OPEN DOOR SPEAKING ENGAGEMENTS

I have had the privilege of telling my story of the school, my mission trips, and my life to many different groups in churches, civic and educational organizations, for example, the Welcome to Savannah group, the Men's Group of the Skidaway Island United Methodist Church, missionary conferences, and Christmas banquets.

HERE AND THERE

Every morning when I get up, I go to my quiet place and read at least four chapters of God's word. I have read the Bible through several times and continue to do that every year. I like to walk to the harbor with my little dog, Tori, go to my bench on the pier where I meet the Lord in prayer, usually at sunrise. I have memorized hundreds of verses of the Bible down through the years.

FAMOUS VISITORS TO OUR WORK

Corrie ten Boom, author of *The Hiding Place*, which is the story of how she survived the Holocaust. She told her story to the students in chapel one day.

Dr. M.R. DeHaan, from the Radio Bible Class in Grand Rapids, Michigan.

Rev. Charles Fuller, of the Fuller Theological Seminary in Pasadena, California.

Mrs. Billy Sunday, the widow of Billy Sunday, the famous evangelist.

Gypsy Smith, the English evangelist, and Arthur McKee, his song-leader.

Mr. and Mrs. Virgil Brock, hymn writers and singers.

Richard Maxwell, who sang on the Columbia Broadcasting System. He always concluded his program with "If I Have Wounded Any Soul Today, Dear Lord Forgive."

Rev. Michael Guido of Metter, Georgia and Joseph Carroll, formerly of Australia, contributed much to the Chapel Services at the school.

Dr. R.A. Forrest of Toccoa Falls Bible College.

Noteworthy Savannah-Area Residents

Among the people who were involved in the early days of the school are the following:

Mr. E.N. Epshaw, the first president of Savannah Christian School.

Ralph Thomas, the architect of all the early buildings.

Hoyt Akins, (no relation to the George Akins), the builder of the early buildings.

E.K. Bell, Olin Fulmer, Herbert Gibbons, Max Hostetter, John Kennedy, Curtis Lewis, Sr., Dr. Newell Turner, *et al.*

Claude Adams, Sam Gardner, Elmo Weeks, D.M. Akins, Hadley B. Cammack, T.H. Guerry, Sr., Dennis Harvey, C.S. Lebey, Jr., George Mayo, G. Walter Mercer, Dr. B.F. Mood, Dr. Claude Moore, Carl W. Seiler, Claude Sills, W. Hughes Smith, Homer L. Strickland, Marcus Stubbs, Edgar R. Terry, Ralph Thomas, T.E. Walker, Benj. B. Williams.

Quotes By Famous Persons And Others

Elvis Presley said, "Sharing money is what gives it its value."

What am I supposed to do after returning from the land of scarcity to the land of plenty where there is so much waste and excess? My roomie, Rita Hill, said, "I know what I'm going to do – hug my toilet." It had gone way up in our estimation after spending time in Kenya.

The Man and the Starfish. I asked the question, "What difference will our small contributions make to the world?" The answer is in this story by an anonymous author. A man was walking along the seashore where starfish had been washed in by the tide. One by one he picked up the starfish and threw them back into the water. A passerby questioned his actions, "Why, are you doing that? There are too many to throw them all back." The man replied, "It makes a big difference to the ones I do throw back."

KEEPSAKES AND MEMORIES

My father's mother, Sally Miller, of South Carolina, was an artist beginning early in her childhood. I have several mementos from her: two pencil drawings done when she was thirteen years of age and a family trunk she took with her when she attended Hollins College in Virginia. The trunk is engraved with the date of 1851.

There is another artist in our family. My younger brother, Fain Griffith, painted the murals on the walls of the guest house at Keesler Air Force Base in Mississippi.

I have some feeble examples of my artwork that leave much to be desired.

Wise Words. When I arrived at Georgia Southern college as a freshman, we were all ushered into the auditorium for a welcoming speech by the registrar, Mr. Joyner. The thought that has remained with me is the following: He said that as children we love people and use things, but as adults we use people and love things.

The first air mail flight to Savannah was a big event in my life. I coaxed Grandpa into taking me. So we went to Hunter Field Army Air Base to witness the arrival of the very first delivery of air mail to the City of Savannah.

Thanks to George, Jr.'s frequent flyer miles and his benevolence I usually flew first class or business class. On my Mission to the World trip to Japan my class was demoted to coach. It was a rude awakening. I was standing at the front of the plane with my coat hanging from my finger. My fellow missionary, Joan, asked "Why are you standing there like that?" I replied, "Waiting for the stewardess to take my coat and hang it up." She said, "Come and sit down, dummy, you're in coach."

John McGinty, one of our personal friends, was headmaster at one time. Melvin Charles was also a headmaster.

Many times worthy students applied for admission but their families were unable to personally pay the tuition. In such cases, either George, Sr. or I would raise the money. For example, we would go to the homes of Christian couples and ask them to provide a scholarship;

George, Sr. at one time raised livestock to be sold and applied to the purchase of additional land.

Words Of Wisdom From Various Authors

I Timothy 4:8. For bodily exercise profiteth little: but godliness is profitable unto all things, having promise of the life that now is, and of that which is to come.

"The older we get, the quicker time goes by."

"If you don't have your priorities right, you will fail.'

"We can't do anything to make the Lord love us more."

"One part of taking piano lessons that I didn't like was playing at recitals."

"We all need goals, but they should be reachable to be achievable."

Guatemalan Twins. When Liselle and Victoria Estrada came to our school at the age of twelve, they did not know a word of English. I immediately became their translator. They were assigned to a sixth grade class to learn English.

One day, the entire class came running into my office and asked me to translate what the twins were saying. The teacher had asked how they made sure children attended school in Guatemala. They pantomimed what looked like shooting an automatic weapon. The students wanted to know if they really shot children who skipped school in Guatemala. After questioning the girls I learned that they didn't shoot them but they did put them in the army.

A Surprise Trip To Branson, Missouri

One day my brother Jack called and said, "Sis, how does a trip to Branson sound?"

Of course, I replied, "Sounds great. When do we go?"

"Tomorrow," he replied.

So, the next day, he, his wife, her sister, and I left on a very rewarding trip to Branson, Missouri.

Another Author In The Family

My brother Fain has just finished a technical book. So now there are two authors in the family.

Support And Encouragement

I would especially like to thank my friend, William J. Glasgow, for his suggestions and invaluable help in the publication of this book.

I would also like to thank Charlie Browning for his assistance.

Thanks also to the following people for their valuable help in setting up my computer system: Debbie Parker, Woody Hale, Fae Kameron, Marsha Moss; and Cindy Fletcher who helped me create an outline of the book.

Charles P. Rowland, a Board Member who paid for George's apppendix operation and hospital stay.

My dear special friends -- Ed and Billie Hale. They are a gift from Heaven.

HAWAII - How I wish I had included my trip with Doris Hurd to the three great islands of Hawaii. Our experience at the Swan Lake Restaurant on Maui was one of the special events that I will always cherish. Each island is different, But magnificent in its own way. Honolulu is to that part of the world what Atlanta is to our part. All flights go through Honolulu. When we stepped off the plane there, a lovely Hawaiian girl placed a lei over our head. We were thus welcomed to the islands. There are several other trips not mentioned.

Mayor Olin Fulmer was one of our Board Members, and very dear to my heart. I knew him to be an outstanding citizen and good churchman. One day when I was praying, God laid on my heart to ask him for an appointment in his office at City Hall, and go witness to him about being born again and having the assurance of a home in Heaven.

How could I possibly dare to do such a thing. However, I called Mayor Fulmer, got the appointment, prayed, and went to his office. He received me graciously, and we had a wonderful discussion about God'd Word. I never mentioned this to anyone.

We entertained the Board in our home for the next meeting. As I was serving the meal, he grabbed my hand and asked permission to tell the men about our meeting. I was so very happy for him to tell about it. It had been a blessing for both of us.

This was not the only time I had orders from above to go witness to men or women. I Thank God for the privilege that was mine.

DAR MEMBERSHIP

I am a member of Lachlan McIntosh Chapter of the Daughters of the American Revolution (DAR).

WHO's WHO

I was listed into the Global Register's Who's Who in Executives and Professionals, as seen in the plaque awarded to me in the 2006-2007 edition of the organization.

I Timothy 1:17
Now unto the King eternal, immortal, invisible, the only wise God, be honor and glory for ever and ever. Amen.